GARMENT
CONSTRUCTION

A Complete Course on
Making Clothing for Fit and Fashion

ILLUSTRATED GUIDE TO SEWING

GARMENT
CONSTRUCTION

A Complete Course on
Making Clothing for Fit and Fashion

BY THE EDITORS AT SKILLS INSTITUTE PRESS

skills institute press

Distributed By
Fox Chapel Publishing

FOX CHAPEL
PUBLISHING

© 2011 by Skills Institute Press LLC
"Illustrated Guide to Sewing" series trademark of Skills Institute Press
Published and distributed in North America by Fox Chapel Publishing Company, Inc., East
Petersburg, PA.

Garment Construction is an original work, first published in 2011.

Portions of text and art previously published by and reproduced under license with Direct
Holdings Americas Inc.

ISBN 978-1-56523-509-0

Library of Congress Cataloging-in-Publication Data

Garment Construction. -- First.
    p. cm. -- (Illustrated guide to sewing.)
Includes index.
ISBN 978-1-56523-509-0
1. Tailoring (Women's) 2. Dressmaking.
TT519.5.G36 2011
646.4'04--dc22
                    2010043122

To learn more about the other great books from Fox Chapel Publishing,
or to find a retailer near you, call toll-free 800-457-9112 or visit us at
www.FoxChapelPublishing.com.

Note to Authors: We are always looking for talented authors to write new books.
Please send a brief letter describing your idea to
Acquisition Editor, 1970 Broad Street, East Petersburg, PA 17520.

Printed in China
First printing: April 2011

Table of Contents

INTRODUCTION

Many people have their first experience with sewing in a junior high home economics class. After several days' worth of incomprehensible lecture, students follow a diagram to thread the machine, and then they sew an apron, a pillow, or a tote bag. Most students check "sewing" off their list of requirements and never pick up a needle again.

With the advent of television decorating shows and reality fashion contests, however, people are rediscovering home sewing. The idea of unique designs is appealing, as is the notion of personally fitted clothes. We have reached a home sewing rennaissance.

Today's home tailors don't want to learn by sewing aprons or pillows, though—nor should they. Most clothing designs are both basic enough for beginners to sew successfully and remarkably similar. If you can master the five classic designs featured in these pages—a simple dress, a tailored shirt, a blouse, a skirt, and pants—you will have the fundamental sewing skills to make almost anything. Conveniently, these five staples are also the building blocks of your wardrobe—items you will make and wear again and again, varying the flourishes and fabric choices to suit your taste as well as changing fashion trends.

LEARNING THE BASICS, PAGE 8

Build a solid foundation for your sewing skills by reviewing the basic tools and techniques.

- Learn machine sewing techniques

- Refresh your hand sewing essentials

- Decide what equipment you really need

- Understand how to choose the best fabric for your figure and your project

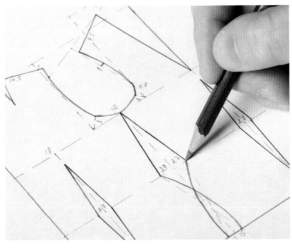

WORKING WITH PATTERNS, PAGE 40

Learn how to choose the perfect pattern for your project, and what to do once you have it.

- Choose the right style and size for your body

- Learn how to measure yourself and which numbers you need to know

- Custom fit a purchased pattern to your measurements

- Use layout and cutting techniques appropriate to your fabric

ASSEMBLING FIVE CLASSIC GARMENTS, PAGE 64

Understanding how to make wardrobe basics will enable you to make any garment.

- Discover the underlying logic in the assembly sequence

- Recognize the role of seams in shaping and fitting a garment

- See how the fit and movement of your clothes depend on a proper sewing process

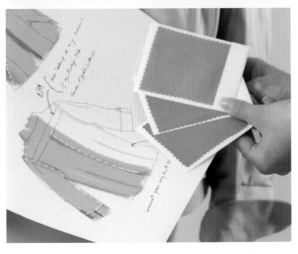

DETAILS OF GARMENT CONSTRUCTION, PAGE 86

Learn professional tailoring methods guaranteed to produce great garments.

- Tackle tricky sleeves, collars, zippers, and waistbands with detailed step-by-step instructions

- Get the details right with expert tips on hems, facings, and fasteners

- Unlock the secrets to perfect pockets, smooth seams, and crisp pleats

- Learn the logic behind darts

LEARNING THE BASICS

1

Before you begin your first sewing project, stop and take stock. Assess your equipment to ensure you have everything you need— you don't want to interrupt your work flow by running to the store for chalk, pins, or thread.

Review your knowledge and experience, as well. Just as certain equipment is essential to success, there are basic techniques that every home sewer must know. Refresh your memory or add to your skills by reviewing the machine and hand stitching instructions on the following pages, as well as the difference between ironing and pressing, cutting techniques, and fabric preparation.

With this solid foundation of equipment and knowledge, you will be ready to choose a pattern and begin sewing classic designs as well as creating your own unique styles.

MACHINE SEWING TECHNIQUES

You may be new to sewing, or perhaps you have been working with a machine for years as a crafter or decorator and have recently decided to learn to sew clothes. Regardless, it makes sense to begin with basic skills. You may learn a new technique, or a tip that is different from, or even more useful than, your standard method. In this chapter, we'll review sewing straight and curved seams, easing, topstitching, and other basic techniques.

If you do not yet own a sewing machine, you will find the marketplace packed with options. There are many brands, styles, and price points, and a plethora of accessories and functions. Your first machine will probably be fairly basic, with features such as variable stitch lengths and styles, buttonhole stitching, and a zipper foot. Your sewing interests are likely to expand, however, so it makes sense to buy a machine that will accommodate your growing ambitions. If you are so inclined, you will find machines that embroider monogramming and pictures, or create intricate quilting stitches.

Regardless of the brand or functions, certain fundamentals concerning needles, thread, and stitching apply to all sewing machines.

- The standard Size 14 needle is suitable for all medium-weight fabrics except knits.
- Knits are best sewn with a Size 14 ballpoint needle.
- The standard thread is No. 50 mercerized cotton or a synthetic.
- Set the machine to sew regular seams at 12 stitches per inch.
- To machine baste, change the seam length setting to six stitches per inch.
- Unless your machine makes stitches designed for knits, they need special procedures (page 17).

For specific instructions on setting up, threading, and operating your sewing machine, see the manual that came with the machine.

Preparing to Sew

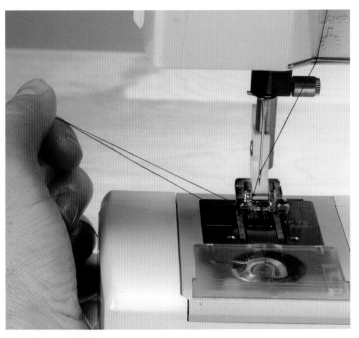

Turn the hand wheel until both the needle and the thread take-up lever are at their highest positions. Pull out 6 inches of thread from the needle and the bobbin.

After Sewing

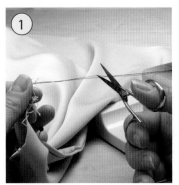

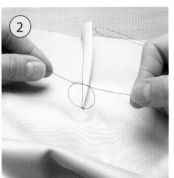

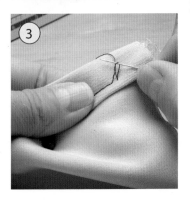

1. Raise the take-up lever to its highest position; raise the presser foot and pull out the fabric. Use the thread cutter on the back of the machine, or scissors, to cut off the needle and bobbin threads.

2. If, when the threads are cut, both are on the same side of the fabric (as on darts), tie a knot close to the stitching and trim the excess with scissors.

3. If, when the threads are cut, one shows on the top, tug the lower thread to pull down a loop from the upper thread. Catch it with a pin and pull it through. Knot and trim.

MACHINE SEWING TECHNIQUES

Sewing a Straight Seam

1. For a permanent seam, lower the needle into the fabric ½ inch from the beginning edge of the seam. Lower the presser foot, reverse the machine and sew backward to the edge. If basting a temporary seam, begin at the edge and do not backstitch.

2. Sew forward from the edge, over the backstitches, then continue along the tracing-wheel markings.

3. Let the machine feed the fabric under the needle by itself; do not pull or push it. Use your hands only to guide and control the fabric along the stitching line.

4. Sew to the edge of the seam. Reinforce permanent seams (not basted ones) by backstitching two or three stitches. Remove the fabric and cut the thread *(After Sewing, page 11)*.

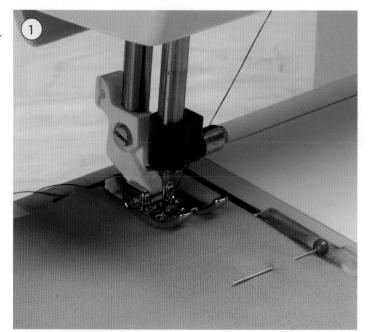

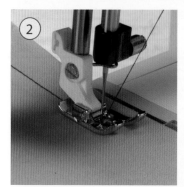

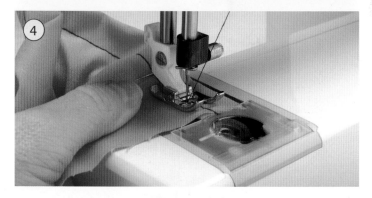

Sewing Right-Angled Corners

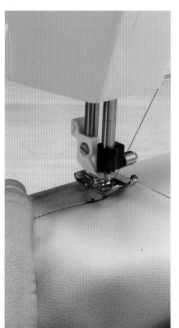
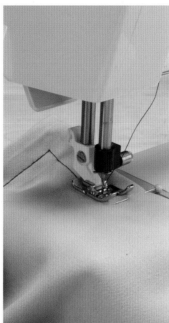

To get around a right-angled corner, sew to the point of the angle. With the needle down into the fabric, raise the presser foot and pivot the fabric 90º. Drop the presser foot again and sew along the other line.

Sewing at Acute Angles

Sew to within one stitch of the point. With the needle down, raise the presser foot and pivot. Make a diagonal stitch, using the hand wheel. Pivot again to sew the other side.

MACHINE SEWING TECHNIQUES

Sewing Around Curves

1. Reinforce curves (such as necklines) after they are cut out, using a row of stay stitching—regular-length stitches sewn ⅟₁₆ inch outside the tracing-wheel markings.

2. When stitching curved seams, guide the fabric around the curve with your hands. Use a slow speed and smaller stitches—about 15 per inch.

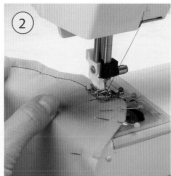

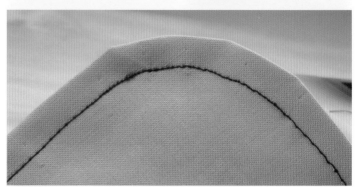

Sewing Eased Seams

Seams that have been eased should be sewn slowly. To prevent a pucker from being stitched down into a pleat, use a seam ripper to flatten out the pucker just before it passes under the needle.

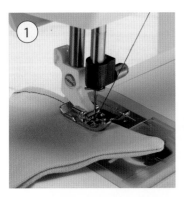

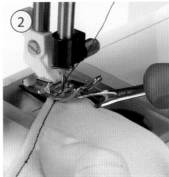

1. Use the presser foot to guide you in edge stitching—sewing a straight line of decorative stitching close to the edge of the fabric. Using a straight-stitch foot, follow the inside edge of its short toe; using an all-purpose foot, follow its right toe.

2. To turn the corner, pause at the point with the needle in the fabric, raise the presser foot and pivot. Push the point under the presser foot with the tip of a seam ripper.

Topstitching

To guide you in topstitching—sewing a straight line of decorative stitching more than ¼ inch in from the fabric edge—use the numbered lines on the throat plate. If the topstitching is to be farther in than ¾ inch from the edge, use the line of edge stitching or a nearby seam as a guide.

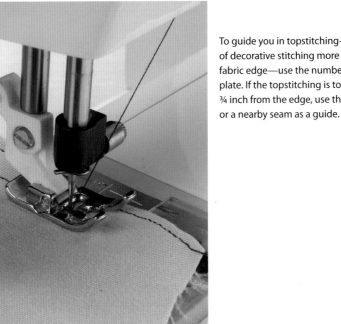

MACHINE SEWING TECHNIQUES

Sewing Zippers

When sewing on a zipper by machine, use the special one-toed zipper foot. Move the foot to the left of the needle if the zipper is to the right, and vice versa, so as to prevent the zipper tab and teeth from interfering with the stitching.

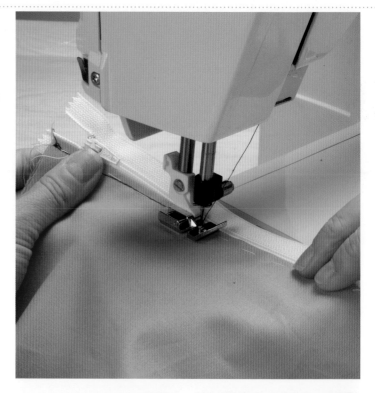

Ripping Out a Line of Stitching

1. On one side of the seam, cut the line of stitching at 1-inch intervals with the cutting edge of a seam ripper.

2. On the other side of the seam, pull out the thread. Pick out the remaining bits of thread.

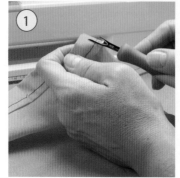

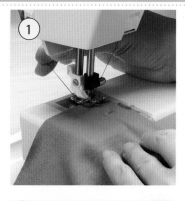

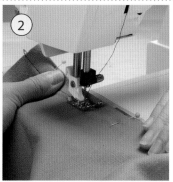

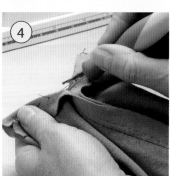

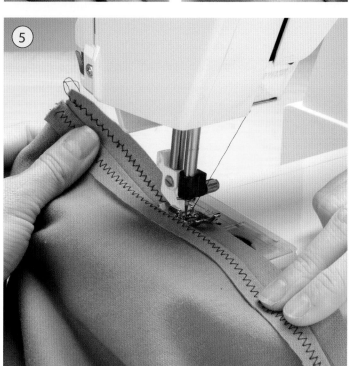

Stitching Knit Fabric

1. After the first stitch, use one hand to pull the knit fabric taut in front of the needle; with your other hand pull the threads in back of the needle.

2. When enough fabric has passed by the needle to grasp from behind, stretch it taut from behind the needle as well as in front. Keep the fabric taut throughout your sewing.

Reinforcing Curved Seams

3. Reinforce curved seams by slowly sewing a row of small stitches—15 per inch—on the stitching line, then sewing a second row ¹⁄₁₆ inch outside the first.

Ripping Out Seams

4. To rip out a seam, spread it open and snip the thread with a seam ripper. Continue spreading and snipping.

Finishing Raw Seams

5. Finish raw seam edges with a zigzag stitch ½ inch in from the seam. Trim.

Chapter 1: LEARNING THE BASICS

No matter how sophisticated your sewing machine, there will always be a time and place for hand stitches—not only temporary basting and marking stitching, but the permanent finishing stitches that can make the difference between an amateur and a professional look.

The easiest sewing tool to select is the thimble; it should be lightweight and fit snugly on your middle finger.

Next, consider the thread, which should be about two shades darker than the fabric color. Mercerized cotton is the most common thread; use it to sew cotton, linen, rayon and cotton-synthetic blends. Silk thread of the type called A is superior for silk, wool, wool-silk blends and synthetics; it is elastic and leaves no lint. Use polyester thread for knits, and silk buttonhole twist for buttons and buttonholes.

Needles are available in 24 sizes—the higher the number, the smaller the needle. The eye must be large enough for thread to pass through freely and the shank must be heavy enough not to bend, but the point must be fine enough to pierce fabric without marring. Use Sizes 7 or 8 for polyester and mercerized thread, Sizes 8 or 9 for silk thread, and 4 or 5 for buttonhole twist.

Simple as they may seem to some, poking the thread through the needle eye and knotting the end securely are often troublesome. The following pages present straightforward methods of accomplishing both fundamental steps.

Sew basting stitches with a single strand of thread no more than 30 inches long. When using them to indicate a stitching line, sew directly on the seam line markings; when basting garment pieces together for fitting purposes, sew a fraction inside or outside the seam line, wherever the stitches will leave no visible trace. On knit fabrics, begin and end basting stitches with a loose fastening stitch. Sew bastings on knits very loosely, and use a shorter stitch length than specified in the instructions that follow.

Make permanent hand stitches with a single strand of thread no more than 18 inches long. Each stitch shown on these pages performs a definite function; the choice of stitch depends on the purpose for which it is intended and the fabric to be sewn.

Threading the Needle

1. Snip off the end of the thread at a 45° angle to give the thread a sharp edge.

2. Hold the needle upright and slightly tilted in one hand so that you can see the eye of the needle clearly. The eye will be even more prominent if the needle is held over a white background. With your other hand push at least ½ inch of the thread through the eye. If the thread does not go through easily, wax it lightly with beeswax to stiffen it.

3. From the other side of the needle, pull the thread through the eye.

Knotting the Thread

1. Loop the end of the thread once around the tip of your index finger to prepare to tie a knot in the end. For a thicker knot that will hold on heavy fabric, loop the thread around your finger two or three times.

2. Roll the loop of thread off your fingertip, keeping the thread taut.

3. With the loop of thread pinched between your thumb and finger, draw it down into a knot.

Using the Thimble

Place the thimble firmly on the middle finger of your sewing hand. Hold the needle between your thumb and forefinger and push it through the material with the side—not the bottom—of the thimble.

Chapter 1: LEARNING THE BASICS

For Markings and Temporary Sewing

1. Using a knotted thread (or in the case of knits, a loose fastening stitch, and in the case of markings, a 4-inch loose end), take a ½-inch stitch in the fabric; pull the thread through.

2. Take another ½-inch stitch ½ inch beyond the first; pull the thread through firmly, but loosely enough not to pucker the fabric. Continue the process.

3. When you are finished, a row of ½-inch stitches will appear on both sides of the piece or pieces of fabric. Secure the end of the line of stitches with a fastening stitch (*opposite*) or leave a 4-inch loose thread, in the case of markings.

4. To remove the basting stitches, first snip the stitch next to the knot, next snip the fastening stitches and then continue to snip at 5-inch intervals; remove the threads. Never pull knots through fabric.

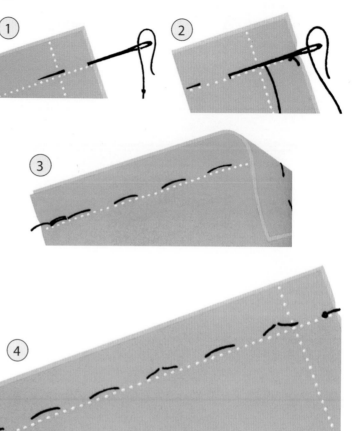

If You are Left-Handed...

Insert the needle as shown; follow the directions in Steps 1–3, proceeding from left to right. Remove the stitches as in Step 4.

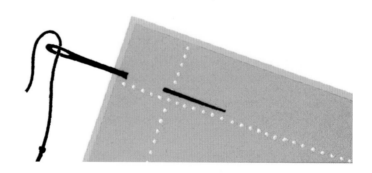

To Mark or Baste Small Areas and to Topstitch

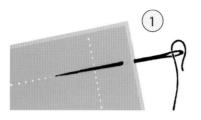

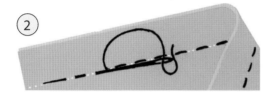

1. Insert the needle through the fabric to be basted or marked and pull the thread through, leaving a loose end 4 inches long; for topstitching, use a knotted thread.

2. Weave the needle in and out of the fabric several times in ⅛-inch, evenly spaced stitches; pull the thread through. Finish with a loose end when marking, and a fastening stitch *(page 28)* on the fabric's wrong side when topstitching.

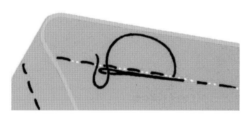

If You are Left-Handed...

Follow the directions in Steps 1 and 2, proceeding from left to right as shown at left.

Chapter 1: LEARNING THE BASICS

For Bound or Raw Edges

1. Anchor the first stitch with a knot inside the hem; then, pointing the needle up and to the left, pick up one or two threads of the garment fabric close to the hem. Push the needle up through the hem ⅛ inch above the edge; pull the thread through.

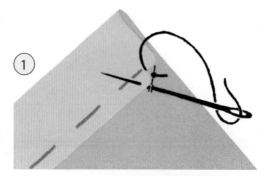

2. Continue the same process—picking up one or two threads, and making ⅛-inch stitches in the hem—at intervals of ¼ inch, creating a tiny slanted stitch on the inside and an almost invisible stitch on the outside. Do not sew too tightly or the fabric will pucker. End with a fastening stitch (page 28).

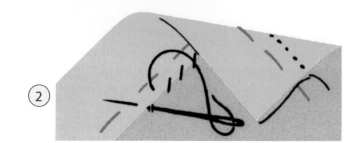

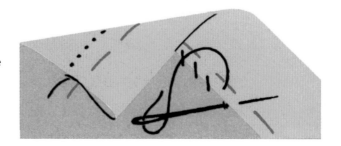

If You are Left-Handed...

Follow the directions in Steps 1 and 2, inserting the needle as shown at right and proceeding from left to right.

For Lightweight Fabrics

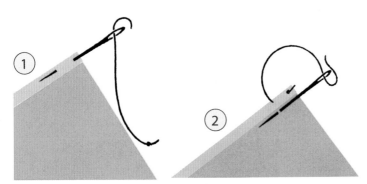

1. Turn the edge of the fabric over ⅛ inch and, using a knotted thread and pointing the needle to the left, make a horizontal stitch ¼ inch long at the top corner of the fold.

2. Pick up one or two threads on the main fabric, below and on a line with the stitch made in Step 1.

3. Take another horizontal stitch in the fold, 1⁄16 inch to the left of the stitch made in Step 1.

4. After repeating Steps 2 and 3 for approximately one inch, hold the sewn section of fabric securely, and gently but firmly pull the thread taut with your other hand. The material will roll over on itself and the stitches will disappear. Continue the rolled-hem stitches, pulling the thread taut every inch and ending with a fastening stitch *(page 28)* hidden in the fold.

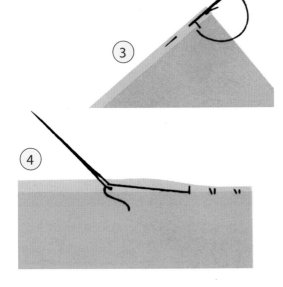

If You are Left-Handed...

Follow the directions in Steps 1–4, inserting the needle as shown at left and proceeding from left to right.

To Hem Knits, Heavy Fabrics

1. Working from left to right, anchor the first stitch with a knot inside the hem ¼ inch down from the edge.

2. Point the needle to the left and pick up one or two threads on the garment close to the top edge of the hem; pull the thread through.

3. Take a small stitch in the top layer only of the hem, ¼ inch down from the edge and ¼ inch to the right of the stitch in Step 2.

4. Continue to pick up a few threads on the garment and to take a small stitch in the hem, creating a triangular pattern on the inside and a line of almost invisible stitches on the side that shows. End with a fastening stitch *(page 28)* on the turned-up hem.

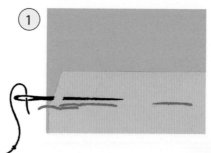

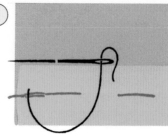

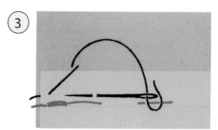

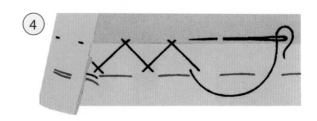

If You are Left-Handed...

Follow the directions in Steps 1–4, proceeding from right to left and pointing the needle to the right, as shown.

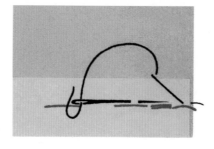

To Hem Folded Edges

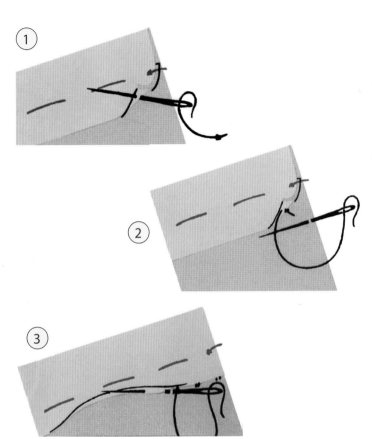

1. Fold under the edge of the hem and anchor the first stitch with a knot inside the fold of the hem.

2. Point the needle to the left and pick up one or two threads of the garment fabric close to the edge of the hem and directly below the stitch made in Step 1.

3. Slide the needle horizontally through the folded edge of the hem ⅛ inch to the left of the previous stitch; the stitches will be almost invisible. Keep the stitches firm but not tight; end with a fastening stitch *(page 28)* inside the fold.

If You are Left-Handed...

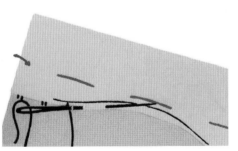

Follow the directions in Steps 1–3, picking up a few threads, then sliding the needle through the folded edge of the hem as shown and proceeding from left to right.

Chapter 1: LEARNING THE BASICS

For Binding Buttonholes

1. Using a knotted thread, insert the needle from the wrong side of the fabric ⅛ inch down from the top edge.

2. Form a loop with the thread by swinging it around in a circle counterclockwise.

3. Insert the needle from the wrong side of the fabric through the same point at which the needle emerged in Step 1, keeping the looped thread under the needle.

4. Draw the thread through, firmly pulling it straight up toward the top edge of the fabric.

5. Repeat Steps 2–4 directly to the left of the first stitch, and continue to make close stitches of even length, forming a firm ridge along the top. End with a fastening stitch *(page 28)* on the wrong side of the fabric.

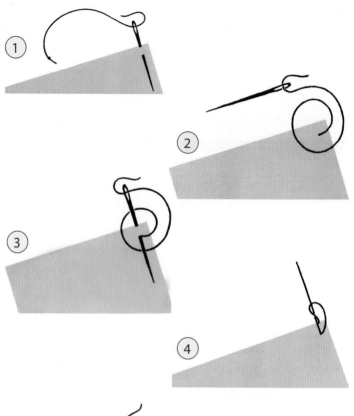

If You are Left-Handed...

Follow the directions in Steps 1–5, proceeding from left to right and looping the thread around the needle as shown.

For Seam Edges

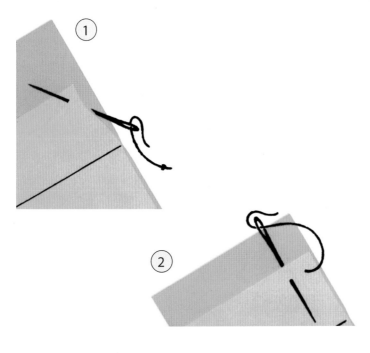

1. Anchor the first stitch with a knot on the wrong side of the fabric and draw the needle through to the other side, ⅛ to ¼ inch down from the top edge.

2. Hold the needle toward you and at a right angle to the fabric. With the thread to the right, insert the needle under the fabric from the wrong side, ⅛ to ¼ inch to the left of the first stitch.

3. Continue to make evenly spaced stitches over the fabric edge. End with a fastening stitch *(page 28)*.

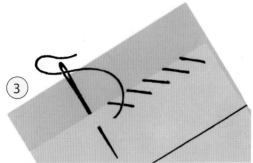

If You are Left-Handed...

Follow the directions in Steps 1–3, proceeding from left to right as shown.

Chapter 1: LEARNING THE BASICS

To Anchor Thread

1. Draw the needle up through the fabric from the wrong side and pull it through.

2. Leaving a 4-inch loose end, insert the needle back ¼ inch. Bring it out at the point at which it first emerged, then pull the thread through.

3. Insert the needle back over the first stitch, and bring it out ¼ inch ahead. After anchoring the thread in this fashion, proceed with the desired stitch.

4. At the end of a row or a length of thread, insert the needle back ¼ inch to the end of the last completed stitch and bring it out at the point at which the thread last emerged.

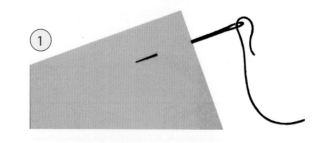

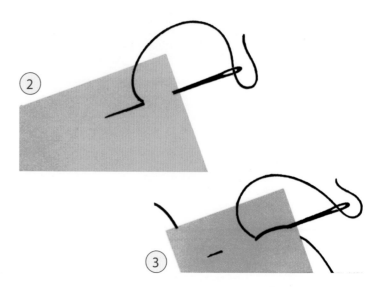

CHAPTER 1: LEARNING THE BASICS

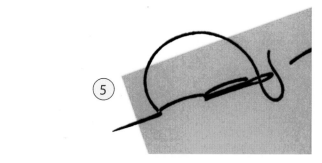

5. Make another stitch directly over the stitch made in Step 4. For extra firmness, repeat again.

6. To remove stitches secured with fastening stitches, first snip the double fastening stitches, then other stitches at 5-inch intervals; pull out the threads.

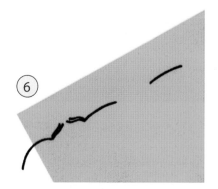

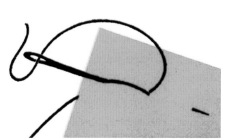

If You are Left-Handed...

Follow the directions in Steps 1–5, proceeding from left to right and inserting the needle as shown at left. Remove the stitches as shown in Step 6.

SEWING EQUIPMENT

Whether you are sewing a simple skirt or a tailored dress, the essential tools are similar, and not numerous: the sewing machine, needles, and thread; pins; scissors; a thimble; and a steam iron.

Of the countless other devices crowding a craft or fabric store, most are needed only for special tasks. However, the following notions are fairly standard and many sewers find them useful:

- A 60-inch tape measure with numbers on both sides is best for body measurements as well as for gauging curved stitching lines. The glass-fiber rather than the cloth or plastic type is preferred; it will not fray or stretch.
- A transparent plastic draftsman's drawing aid, called a French curve, that enables you to trace smooth curves instead of drawing them freehand is also handy.
- A 2- by 18-inch transparent plastic ruler should be available for short measurements, as well as a yardstick for longer ones.

- You will also want pressing cloths of both the see-through and thick cotton varieties, as well as a sleeveboard for ironing sleeves.
- One useful gadget is an emery bag—a small pincushion that contains abrasives similar to those used for sharpening knives. Pins and needles are quickly sharpened when thrust in and out of it.
- You will need a pair of pointed, 4-inch scissors for cutting buttonholes, snipping thread and other small jobs.

Even minimal space need not interfere with efficient—and attractive—storage of sewing gear. A plastic silverware tray, for example, can simultaneously store and display your spools of thread. If the spools are laid on their sides, colors are instantly identifiable. Large clear plastic boxes can hold patterns separated by identifying index cards. Wicker baskets serve as handsome containers for materials. (Remember to line a hamper to prevent snagging.) And an old trunk is another capacious receptacle for fabrics, while paper or tin boxes hold notions.

Use the iron as soon as you begin a project, to smooth the material and pattern. The secret of perfect ironing is to glide, not push, the iron forward.

Pressing is a very different technique, used to flatten details such as pleats or seams, as soon as they are permanently sewn. The trick here is to set the iron down vertically, directly on the spot to be pressed.

It is easier to press a seam during the sewing process than it is to wait until later, when the iron must be wiggled into the corners of the completed garment. A combination steam-dry iron is best.

Final ironing and pressing are done on the right side of the fabric (the side that is visible in the completed garment). Use a cloth over the material to protect it from scorching or from developing a shine—a silicone cloth for heavy fabrics and cheesecloth for lightweight materials. To get the right ironing temperature, it is a good idea to experiment with a swatch of extra material.

Ironing

Use a long, gliding, forward motion. Try not to move the iron backward—you might put wrinkles back in.

Pressing

Set the iron straight down on the material with even pressure; lift it straight up.

Detail Pressing

With your free hand, open up angles and folds in the fabric. Use only the point of the iron to press confined spaces.

Three basic scissors will see you through every step of making most garments:

• Cut out the pattern with 8- or 10-inch bent-handled dressmakers shears.

• Clip curves and small areas with 6-inch scissors.

• Finish raw seam edges by trimming with pinking shears, which have zigzag teeth.

For long, straight cuts, a rotary cutter is useful. Shaped like a pizza cutter, the sharpened wheel slices through single and double layers of fabric quickly and easily. To ensure straight lines, use a plastic ruler as a cutting guide. To avoid dulling the blade, always cut on a plastic mat designed for use with a rotary cutter.

Straight Lines

Open the shears wide and take in fabric the whole length of the blades. Cut with one long steady closure for a smooth edge.

Curves

Open the shears halfway and never quite close them as you cut around a curve. This will make an arc instead of a series of a jagged lines.

Right Angles

Cut two intersecting straight lines by cutting along one marked line, then pulling the shears out and cutting along the second line at the point at which the two meet. This produces a crisp, true angle instead of a swivel.

Clipping

Clip into curves and small details with the tips of 6-inch scissors. Do not open them all the way; you can more easily see how far to clip if you use only the tips.

Pinking

Finish seam edges on any fabric but knits by pinking them; open the shears wide and close them smoothly.

Rotary Cutter

Place a cutting mat on your work surface, marked side up. Lay the fabric on the mat, aligning two sides with two intersecting lines of the mat. Place a plastic ruler on the fabric, aligning it with either pattern pieces or guidelines on the mat, and hold it in place with one hand. Using the other hand, push the trigger on the rotary cutter, set it against the ruler, and press firmly while rolling the cutter along the ruler edge. Start and end your cut on the mat, off the edge of the fabric.

Chapter 1: LEARNING THE BASICS

Although you may be tempted to grab a piece of fabric and begin immediately, it pays to spend a little time choosing the best piece of material for your project and properly preparing it for the sewing process.

One of the joys of sewing your own clothes is creatively pairing fabrics with pattern styles. However, you will find that your finished garments are more flattering when the weight and type of fabric coordinate with the pattern. Medium-weight flannel, for instance, makes up into a nice skirt or pants, but something softer, like a silky cotton, is better for a blouse, and a jersey knit drapes nicely for a dress. Most pattern envelopes include fabric suggestions.

You will also want to choose fabrics that work well on your body—colors and designs that complement your figure and complexion. The chart opposite includes basic principles of color and pattern theory that will help you choose appropriate fabrics.

Once you purchase fabric, it is essential that you shrink it before cutting, unless it is preshrunk and has a label that says so. If the material is nonwashable, take it to a dry cleaner to be shrunk. If it is washable, follow the instructions on page 37, Step 14.

An equally important preparatory step is straightening the fabric. If it was stretched out of shape prior to being placed on the bolt, or if it was not cut on the true grain—that is, with the lengthwise and crosswise threads at right angles to each other—the finished garment will not fit properly or hang evenly. Straightening the fabric corrects those issues.

In general, natural fibers are more easily cut on the true grain than synthetics and, even if slightly off, are easier to adjust. Synthetic fabrics and those that are a mixture of natural and synthetic fibers may need more straightening. Both can be adjusted by following the instructions on the following pages for aligning the crosswise and lengthwise, or selvage, edges.

It's been said that the perfect garment is a marriage between the right style and the right fabric. Choosing an appropriate color, pattern, and weight of fabric can make the difference between a successful outfit and one that is not flattering.

The color and weight of a fabric can make the wearer look larger or smaller, depending on the tone and whether the fabric drapes against the body or stands away from it. Pattern—whether large, small, regular, or random—is also vital. Below are several factors to consider when choosing fabrics for sewing projects.

Chapter 1: LEARNING THE BASICS

Warm Colors

Warm colors, such as red and orange, tend to exaggerate the size of the body and can make even a slender person appear more voluptuous—especially when the color is used lavishly in a long garment. The enlarging effect diminishes, however, in a short dress, and becomes so minimal in a bikini that it could safely be worn on an ample figure.

Cool Colors

Cool colors, such as blue and green, minimize the dimensions of a figure so that they produce a soft, even fragile, effect on a slim body. On a large person, they can create the impression that the figure is closer to ideal proportions. As with warm colors, cool ones become more effective as the quantity of fabric increases.

Vertical Stripes

Vertical stripes generally make the wearer look taller and slimmer. In a simple dress, wide stripes give a dramatic illusion of greater height. However, in a more detailed dress, such as one with a waistband, yoke, or collar, the same wide stripes become a detriment by making the garment appear too busy. In contrast, a detailed dress made in narrow stripes recaptures the impression of slimness. Vertical stripes also give a tailored appearance.

Horizontal Stripes

Horizontal stripes appear to make the wearer look broader and shorter. The illusion is most marked when the stripes are both wide and warm in color. This effect of breadth can be minimized by using the stripe in a cool color, or a narrow stripe of any color.

Patterns

Patterns can draw bold attention to a figure, in either a positive or negative way. Large-scale prints can make a body appear larger, as can small prints in bright colors. Geometric prints that run vertically can, like stripes, make the wearer appear taller. Circular patterns create a softer, more fluid look than stripes or other geometric shapes.

Plaids and Checks

Plaids and checks pose few figure problems if the patterns are small and cut so they run vertically and horizontally. Bold plaid can make the body look larger, but cutting them on the diagonal minimizes this effect.

Textures

Textures differ so dramatically that they create a variety of effects even when made in identical styles. Soft, clinging knits give an alluring look, while a crisp fabric like cotton duck looks sporty. Mohair, having more nap, can make the wearer's figure seem fuller.

Finding the Crosswise Grain Line

1. Iron the fabric on the wrong side to remove wrinkles and any lines made by folding.

2. If your fabric is knit, skip to Step 8. If your fabric is woven, spread it wrong side up on a flat surface. Snip into the selvage (lengthwise) edge near one end, at a point where a single thread runs the entire width of the material.

3. Using a pin, snag a crosswise thread from the snipped edge.

4. Pull gently on the thread, easing it along as though you were gathering the fabric; the pulled thread will show up as a puckered line.

5. If the pulled thread breaks as you pull it, cut along the pulled line to the point of the break and pick up the same or nearest crosswise thread. Continue to pull the thread.

6. Cut along the pulled line from one selvage through to the other; this is the true crosswise grain.

7. Repeat Steps 1–6 at the opposite end of the fabric.

8. If your fabric is knit, place an L-shaped square near one crosswise edge of the fabric. Align one side of the square with a selvage edge.

9. Draw a chalk line along the crosswise grain of the fabric at a right angle to the selvage.

10. Cut along the chalk line from one selvage to the other.

11. Repeat Steps 8–10 at the opposite end of the fabric.

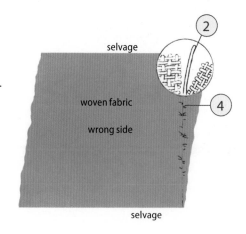

selvage

woven fabric

wrong side

selvage

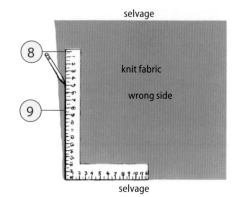

selvage

knit fabric

wrong side

selvage

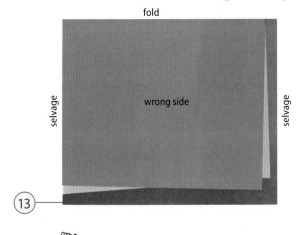

12. Fold the fabric in half lengthwise, wrong sides facing outward, and carefully match the selvages.

13. Place the folded fabric on a flat surface that has right-angled corners, such as a table top. Align the selvages against one edge of the table and the raw crosswise edges against the other. If the raw edges do not match evenly and the corners do not form perfect right angles, the fabric is off grain and needs straightening.

Straightening the Fabric

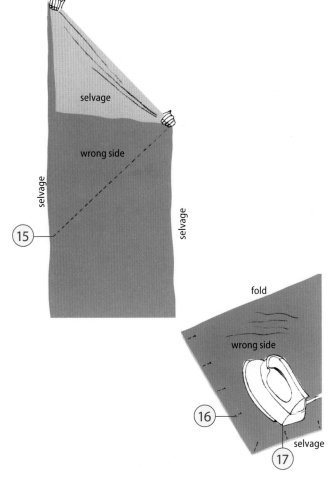

14. If your fabric is not washable, skip to Step 16. Fold the fabric in loose pleats and immerse it for about an hour in a sink with water at the temperature recommended for the material. Then gently squeeze out the water and lay the fabric on a flat surface until it is slightly dry. (For best results, do *not* use an automatic dryer.)

15. To straighten the damp fabric, begin by folding the material so that the selvage falls horizontally as shown. Grasp one corner and a point on the material as far along the diagonally opposite edge as you can reach. Pull hard. Repeat by sliding the hand at the corner down to the point of the original fold and again place the other hand as far along the opposite edge as you can reach. Continue this process until you have stretched the entire piece of fabric.

16. Fold the fabric in half lengthwise with wrong sides facing out and pin together the crosswise edges and the selvages at 5-inch intervals, using rust-proof pins. As you pin, smooth the fabric toward the fold with your hands.

17. Using a steam iron, begin to iron at the pinned selvage edges and move toward the fold. Continue moving in parallel paths until you have ironed the complete length of the material.

Folding Solid Fabric

1. For most patterns, fold your fabric in half lengthwise so that it is wrong side out. This layout conserves fabric and enables you to position all at once as many pattern pieces as you need. Pin the selvages together at 1- to 2-inch intervals.

2. For pattern pieces that are too wide to be cut on fabric folded lengthwise, fold the fabric in half crosswise so that it is wrong side out.

3. If your cutting guide requires some pieces to be cut from a double and some from a single thickness of fabric, fold all the fabric as shown in Step 1 or 2, depending on the cutting guide instructions, and cut out all the pieces requiring double thicknesses. Then spread the rest of the material out in a single thickness, wrong side down.

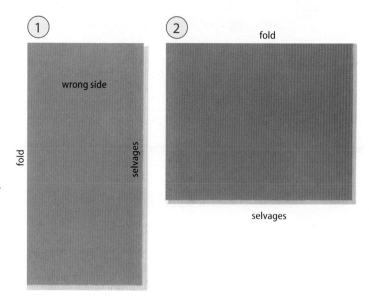

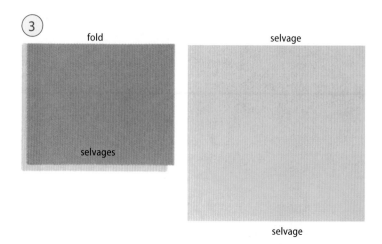

Folding Striped or Checked Fabric

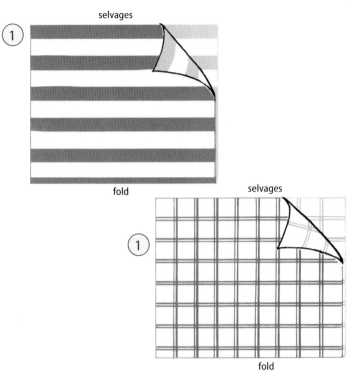

1. If the fabric has stripes or checks of similar size, fold it so that the fold line falls exactly halfway through a stripe or check.

2. Starting near the fold and working to the selvages, stick pins through the top layer of fabric where check lines intersect (or at the edge of stripe lines).

3. Fold back the top layer and make sure that the pins bring together the two layers at points where the pattern matches exactly. If the pattern does not match, adjust the fabric.

4. Catch the point of the pin to hold the layers together. Continue inserting pins in this manner at a number of points. Then pin the fabric together at the edges.

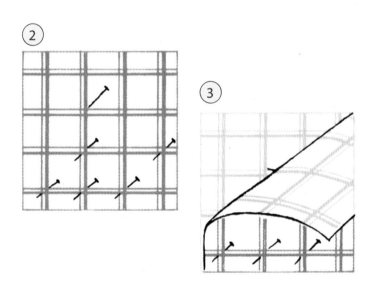

WORKING WITH PATTERNS

The key to making clothes that will suit you lies in choosing pattern lines and fabric colors, weights and textures properly proportioned to one another and to the scale of your figure.

Do not rely on measurements alone to analyze your figure. You should also stand in front of a full-length three-way mirror, preferably in a revealing bathing suit or leotard, and examine your figure from all angles.

Then, with your own image firmly in mind, choose a pattern that emphasizes your good features while drawing attention away from the others. For example, an empire waistline nicely accentuates a small-busted, trim-shouldered figure, and conceals a prominent bottom. Pleated and gathered skirts can pad out hips that are slim, but they make heavy hips even more noticeable.

Visualizing how a silhouette will look on you can be difficult. An excellent way to find out—and a good deal of fun—is to go to the "better dresses" department in a store and try on outfits until you find the styles that are most becoming. Then select a pattern that has the same silhouette and lines.

Once you choose a style, buy the pattern that most closely matches your measurements (pages 43 and 45). Then follow the instructions on pages 46 to 57 to custom fit the pattern to your body, ensuring that your finished garment is as comfortable and flattering as possible.

Women's patterns are much more rigidly standardized than ready-to-wear clothes, so your ordinary dress size is not a reliable guide to the correct pattern size. Pattern sizes are divided into five figure types, based on measurements. The Misses type is considered average; others are based on different heights and proportions. Men's patterns are all based on the average male figure.

To determine your figure type, first note your measurements, shown by red bands on the figures at right. Find your height in the charts on page 45, and then look for any special characteristics in the descriptions, such as narrow shoulders or a high bust. Select the categories that best describe your overall figure, then compare the measurements for bust and hip. Use these dimensions to make the final selection; ignore pattern labels, such as Women or Junior, which are intended to describe figure type, not age.

Within your figure type, choose the size nearest your horizontal measurements. (Vertical measurements are easier to adjust.) For dresses and shirts, be guided by bust size; for skirts and pants, hip size. (If the circumference of your body at the thighs, abdomen or buttocks exceeds that at your hips, use the larger dimension to determine size.)

If all measurements fall between sizes, take the smaller size if you are small-boned, the larger if big-boned.

Measure yourself with a tape held snugly against the body. The red lines on the figures below indicate measurements on pattern envelopes; the blue lines are additional measurements for further fitting. Wear the underwear and shoes that you will wear with the finished garment.

1. Height: Stand erect, without shoes, against a wall. Place a ruler flat on your head and mark the point where the ruler touches the wall. Measure from the mark to the floor.

2. Bust: Measure around the fullest part with the tape slightly raised in back.

3. Waist: Tie a cord around the narrowest part; measure around from behind. Leave the cord for other measurements.

4. Full Hip: Measure from behind around the fullest part, usually 7 to 9 inches down from the waist.

5. Back-Waist Length: Measure from the top of the spine to the waistline cord.

6. Arm Length: Measure from the shoulder-bone point to the elbow. With the elbow bent, measure under the elbow to the wristbone.

7. Crotch Length: Sitting on a hard surface, measure from the waistline cord to the surface.

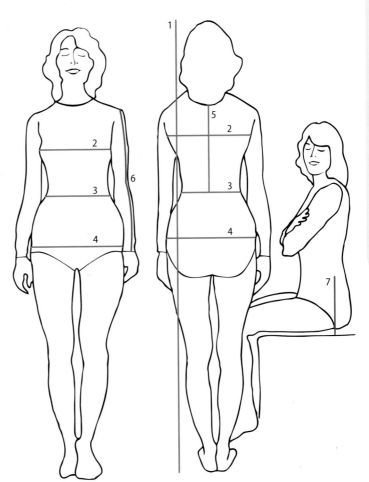

1. Height: Measure as for women.

2. Neck: From about an inch above the top of the spine, measure around the neck.

3. Chest: With the chest slightly expanded, measure from the shoulder blades across the fullest part, with the tape under the armpits.

4. Sleeve Length: Measure from the top of the spine across to the shoulder-bone point, then down to the elbow. Bend the arm to a right angle and measure from under the elbow to the wrist.

5. Arm Length: Measure as for women.

6. Waist: Start at the navel and measure around the body.

7. Hip or Seat: Measure at the widest part of the hips or buttocks and at the midpoint of the pelvic bone.

8. Crotch: Measure from the waistline cord as for woman.

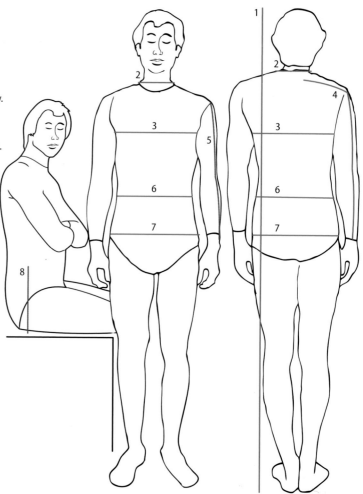

Misses

Designed for the female American figure of average proportions, 5'5" to 5'6" tall without shoes.

Size	6	8	10	12	14	16	18	20
bust	30½"	31½"	32½"	34"	36"	38"	40"	42"
waist	23"	24"	25"	26½"	28"	30"	32"	34"
hip	32½"	33½"	34½"	36"	38"	40"	42"	44"
back-waist length	15½"	15¾"	16"	16¼"	16½"	16¾"	17"	17¼"

Miss Petite

Designed for figures 5'2" to 5'4" tall without shoes, with back-waist lengths shorter than Misses.

Size	6MP	8MP	10MP	12MP	14MP	16MP
bust	30½"	31½"	32½"	34"	36"	38"
waist	23½"	24½"	25½"	27"	28½"	30½"
hip	32½"	33½"	34½"	36"	38"	40"
back-waist length	14½"	14¾"	15"	15¼"	15½"	15¾"

Women

Designed for figures 5'5" to 5'6" tall without shoes, with larger bust and hips than the Misses figure.

Size	38	40	42	44	46	48	50
bust	42"	44"	46"	48"	50"	52"	54"
waist	35"	37"	39"	41½"	44"	46½"	49"
hip	44"	46"	48"	50"	52"	54"	56"
back-waist length	17¼"	17⅜"	17½"	17⅝"	17¾"	17⅞"	18"

Juniors'

Juniors' are for the young miss figure, about 5'2" to 5'5" in height without shoes.

Measurements in Inches

Size	3/4	5/6	7/8	9/10	11/12	13/14	15/16	17/18
bust	28	29	30½	32	33½	35	36½	38½
waist	22	23	24	25	26	27	28	29½
hip	31	32	33½	35	36½	38	39½	41½
back-waist length	13½	14	14½	15	15⅜	15¾	16⅛	16¾

Men

Designed for the male American figure of average proportions, 5'10" tall without shoes.

Size	34	36	38	40	42	44	46	48
chest	34"	36"	38"	40"	42"	44"	46"	48"
waist	28"	30"	32"	34"	36"	39"	42"	44"
hip (seat)	35"	37"	39"	41"	43"	45"	47"	49"
neckband	14"	14½"	15"	15½"	16"	16½"	17"	17½"
shirt sleeve	32"	32"	33"	33"	34"	34"	35"	35"

ADJUSTING PATTERNS

Few figures are so perfectly proportioned that they match all the body measurements on which a pattern is based. The time to check your measurements against those on the pattern envelope is before you cut, while you can still adjust the pattern.

How you adjust the pattern is important. It is tempting just to cut the fabric a little wider at the hips or to add an inch or so at the hem. But unless adjustments are made at the right spot, the lines of the garment will be ruined.

See how your measurements differ from those for which the pattern was designed—they are printed on the pattern envelope—and make any necessary adjustments on the basis of these differences. Do not compare your measurements with the dimensions of the pattern pieces themselves; *most* pieces allow extra room for comfort and style. Sleeve, crotch and hem lengths, however, are exceptions; here you can compare your measurements directly with the pattern pieces.

Before you adjust, trim your pattern close to the cutting line and iron each piece with a warm, dry iron. Work first on vertical adjustments, then on the horizontal ones; mark all measurement changes on the pattern piece and then draw new cutting and stitching lines as shown on the following pages.

Basic Steps for Lengthening

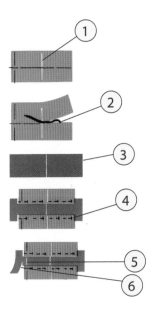

1. Draw a pencil line *(white)* at a right angle to the adjustment line marked on your pattern for lengthening or shortening. The pencil line should extend about 2 inches above and below the adjustment line.

2. Cut the pattern along the adjustment line.

3. Cut out a piece of shelf paper slightly wider than the pattern section you are working on and about 6 inches high; draw a vertical line through its center.

4. Pin the shelf paper to the cut-apart pattern so that the vertical lines are aligned and the pattern pieces are separated by the exact amount the section is to be lengthened.

5. Draw a new stitching line *(white)*, tapering it into the original stitching line.

6. Mark and trim a new cutting edge ⅝ inch outside the new stitching line.

Lengthening at the Waistline

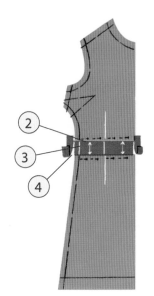

1. For a one-piece dress, compare your back-waist length measurement *(page 43)* with the measurement printed on the pattern envelope. If your measurement is longer than specified, lengthen the pattern at the waist before you set the hem length.

2. Add the pattern insert as shown in the basic steps for lengthening, working on the front section of your pattern.

3. Extend the stitching line *(white)* of the side seam across the pattern insert; taper it into the original stitching line, a few inches above and below the insert, making a smooth line from the seam intersection at the dart or armhole down to the intersection of the original stitching line and the bottom of the pattern piece.

4. Mark and trim a new cutting edge ⅝ inch outside the new stitching line.

5. Repeat on the back section of your pattern.

ADJUSTING PATTERNS: LENGTHENING

Lengthening the Lower Portion of a Garment

1a. For a dress or a skirt, measure from your center front waistline the desired length of the garment. Mark the length on the center front of the pattern. This step should be done after any necessary lengthening or shortening at the waist.

1b. For pants, mark your pants length measurement on the side seam of the pattern piece. This step should be done after any necessary lengthening or shortening at the crotch.

2. If the mark is below the hemline indicated on the skirt or pants pattern, you will have to lengthen the pattern by an amount equal to the difference between your mark and the original hemline.

3. Add the pattern insert as shown in the basic steps for lengthening, working on the front section of your pattern.

4. Extend the stitching line *(white)* of the side seam across the pattern insert. Taper this line into the original stitching line, a few inches above and below the insert, making a smooth line from the side seam at the waistline down to the intersection of the original stitching line and the bottom of the pattern piece.

5. Mark and trim a new cutting edge ⅝ inch outside the new stitching line.

6. Repeat on the back section of your pattern.

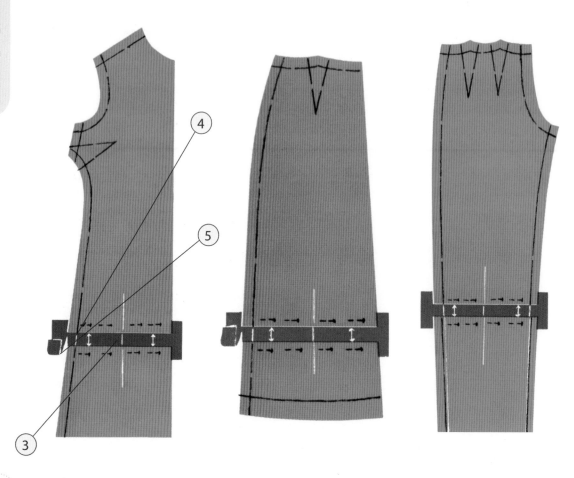

Lengthening at the Crotch

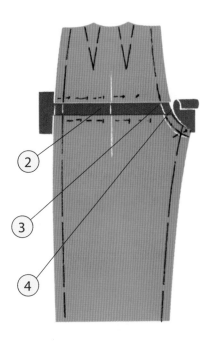

1. For pants, compare your crotch length measurement *(pages 43–44)* with the pattern's, measuring along the side of the pattern from the waist seam allowance to a point opposite the bottom of the crotch seam allowance. If your measurement is longer than the pattern's, you will have to lengthen the pattern at the crotch before you set the hem length.

2. Add the pattern insert as shown in the basic steps for lengthening, working on the front section of your pattern.

3. Extend the stitching line *(white)* across the pattern insert. Taper this line into the original stitching line, a few inches above and below the insert, making a smooth line from the waistline down to the intersection of the crotch seam and the inner leg seam.

4. Mark and trim a new cutting edge ⅝ inch outside the new stitching line.

5. Repeat on the back section of your pattern.

Lengthening a Sleeve

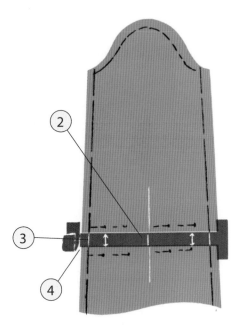

1. Compare your arm length measurement *(pages 43–44)* with the pattern piece measurement, measuring from the center of the seam allowance at the top of the sleeve to the hemline. If your measurement is longer than the pattern's, you will have to lengthen the pattern.

2. Add the pattern insert as shown in the basic steps for lengthening.

3. Extend the stitching lines *(white)* of the underarm seam across the pattern insert, working on both sides of the pattern piece. Taper these lines into the original stitching lines, a few inches above and below the insert, making smooth lines from the intersection of the underarm seams and the armhole seam down to the intersection of the original stitching lines and the bottom of the pattern piece.

4. Mark and trim a new cutting edge ⅝ inch outside the new stitching line.

Basic Steps for Shortening

1. Draw a line *(white)* above the adjustment line marked on your pattern for lengthening or shortening. The distance should be exactly equal to the amount the pattern section is to be shortened.

2. Fold the pattern so that the adjustment line meets the new line.

3. Press the fold flat with a warm iron.

4. Pin a paper extension to your pattern.

5. Draw a new stitching line *(white)*, tapering it into the original stitching line.

6. Mark and trim a new cutting edge ⅝ inch outside the new stitching line.

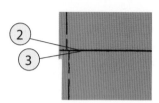

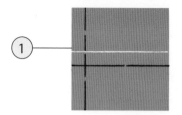

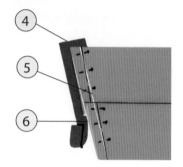

Shortening at the Waistline

1. For a one-piece dress, compare your back-waist length measurement *(page 43)* with the measurement printed on the pattern envelope. If your measurement is shorter than specified, shorten the pattern at the waist before you set the hem length.

2. Fold and extend the pattern as shown in the basic steps for shortening, working on the front section of your pattern.

3. Draw a new stitching line *(white)* across the folded pattern piece and extension. Taper this line into the original stitching line of the side seam, a few inches above and below the fold, making a smooth line from the seam intersection at the dart or armhole to the intersection of the original stitching line and the bottom of the pattern.

4. Mark and trim a new cutting edge ⅝ inch outside the new stitching line.

5. Repeat on the back section of your pattern.

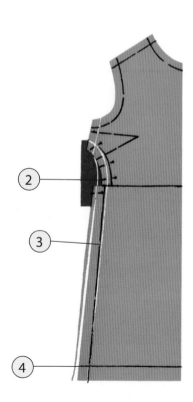

Shortening the Lower Portion of a Garment

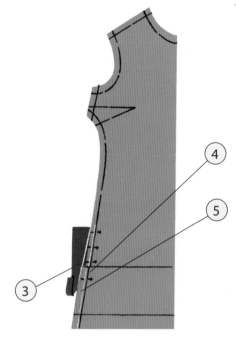

1a. For a dress or a skirt, measure from your waistline the desired length of the garment. Mark the length on the pattern. This step should be done after any necessary lengthening or shortening at the waist.

1b. For pants, mark your pants length measurement on the side seam of the pattern piece. This step should be done after any necessary lengthening or shortening at the crotch.

2. If your mark is above the hemline indicated on the pattern, shorten the pattern by an amount equal to the difference between your mark and the original hemline.

3. Fold and extend the pattern as shown in the basic steps for shortening, working on the front section of your pattern.

4. Draw a new stitching line (white) across the folded pattern piece and the extension. Taper this line into the original stitching line, a few inches above and below the fold, making a smooth line from the side seam at the waistline down to the intersection of the original stitching line and the bottom of the pattern.

5. Mark and trim a new cutting edge ⅝ inch outside the new stitching line.

6. Repeat on the back section of your pattern.

ADJUSTING PATTERNS: SHORTENING

Shortening at the Crotch

1. For pants, compare your crotch length measurement *(pages 43–44)* with the pattern's, measuring from the waist seam allowance to a point opposite the bottom of the crotch seam allowance. If your measurement is shorter than the pattern's, shorten the pattern at the crotch before you set the hem length.

2. Fold and extend the pattern as shown in the basic steps for shortening, working on the front section of your pattern.

3. Draw a new stitching line *(white)* across the folded pattern piece and the extension. Taper this line into the original stitching line for the crotch seam, a few inches above and below the fold, making a smooth line from the waistline to the intersection of the crotch seam and the inner leg seam.

4. Mark and trim a new cutting edge ⅝ inch outside the new stitching line.

5. Repeat on the back section of your pattern.

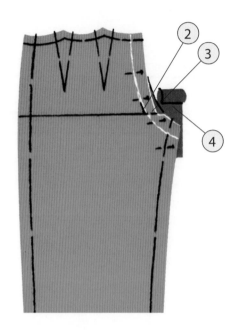

Shortening a Sleeve

1. Compare your arm length measurement *(pages 43–44)* with the pattern piece measurement, measuring from the center of the seam allowance at the top of the sleeve to the hemline. If your measurement is shorter than the pattern's, you will have to shorten the pattern.

2. Fold and extend the pattern as shown in the basic steps for shortening.

3. Extend the stitching lines *(white)* for the underarm seam across the folded pattern piece and the extension, working on both sides of the pattern piece. Taper these new lines into the original stitching lines, a few inches above and below the fold, making smooth lines from the intersection of the underarm seams and the armhole seams down to the intersection of the original stitching lines and the bottom of the pattern piece.

4. Mark and trim a new cutting edge ⅝ inch outside the new stitching line.

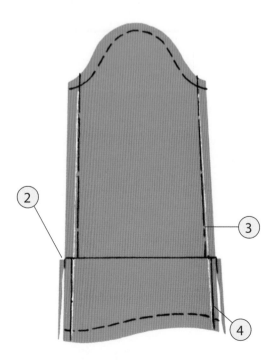

Basic Steps for Enlarging

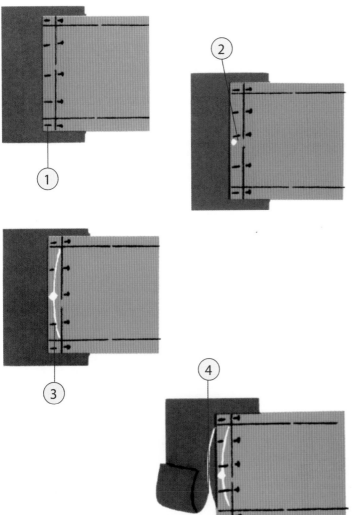

1. Lay your pattern piece on a strip of shelf paper cut to extend about 2 inches underneath the pattern and about 2 inches beyond the edge. Pin the pattern to the shelf paper.

2. At the point where you need to enlarge your pattern piece, measure out from the stitching line and mark *(white)* ¼ of the total amount to be enlarged on each seam. Measure onto the seam allowance—or beyond it onto the shelf paper, if necessary.

3. Draw a new tapered stitching line *(white)* from the point of enlargement into the original stitching line.

4. Mark and trim a new cutting edge ⅝ inch outside the new stitching line.

ADJUSTING PATTERNS: ENLARGING

Enlarging at the Waistline

1. For a one-piece dress, a skirt or pants, compare your waist measurement *(pages 43–44)* with that printed on the pattern envelope. If your measurement is larger than specified, you will have to enlarge the pattern at the waist.

2. Working on the front section of your pattern, extend the pattern as shown in the basic steps for enlarging.

3. Measure out and mark as shown *(white)* ¼ of the amount to be enlarged on each side seam.

4. Mark as shown *(white)* the location of the fullest part of your hips.

5. Draw a new stitching line, starting at the waistline mark made in Step 3 and tapering it into the original stitching line. Come as close as possible to the hipline mark made in Step 4 while maintaining the original contour of the pattern's stitching line. For a dress, extend the new stitching line above the waistline, tapering it into the dart or armhole seam.

6. Mark and trim a new cutting edge ⅝ inch outside the new stitching line.

7. Repeat on the back section of your pattern.

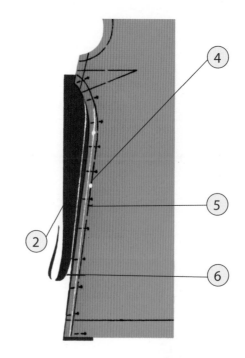

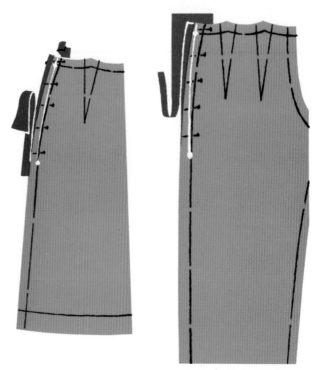

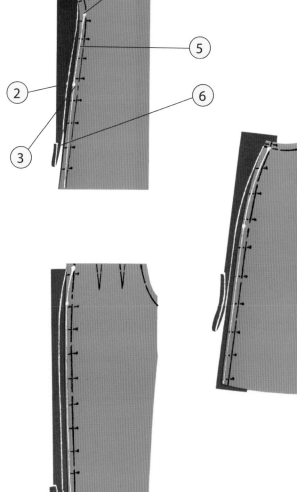

1. For a one-piece dress, a skirt or pants, compare your hip measurement *(pages 43–44)* with that printed on the pattern envelope. If your measurement is larger than specified, enlarge the pattern at the hips.

2. Working on the front section of your pattern, extend the pattern as shown in the basic steps for enlarging.

3. Measure out and mark as shown *(white)* ¼ of the amount to be enlarged on each side seam.

4. Mark as shown *(white)* the location of your waistline.

5. Draw a new tapered stitching line from the waistline marking made in Step 4 to the new hipline marking made in Step 3; then continue in a line parallel to the original stitching line down to the bottom of the pattern piece.

6. Mark and trim a new cutting edge ⅝ inch outside the new stitching line.

7. Repeat on the back section of your pattern.

Chapter 2: WORKING WITH PATTERNS

Basic Steps for Reducing

1. At the point where you need to reduce your pattern piece, measure in from the stitching line and mark *(white)* ¼ of the total amount to be reduced on each side seam.

2. Draw a new stitching line *(white)* making a graduated curve from the point of reduction to the original stitching line.

3. Mark and trim a new cutting edge ⅝ inch outside the new stitching line.

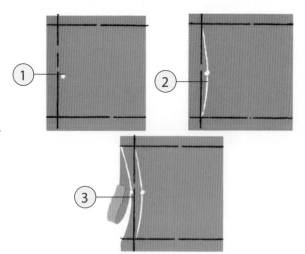

Reducing at the Waistline

1. For a one-piece dress, a skirt or pants, compare your waist measurement *(pages 43–44)* with that printed on the pattern envelope. If your measurement is less than specified you will have to reduce the pattern at the waist.

2. Working on the front section of your pattern, measure in and mark as shown ¼ of the amount to be reduced on each side seam.

3. Mark as shown *(white)* the location of the fullest part of your hips.

4. Draw a new tapered stitching line, starting at the new waistline mark made in Step 2 and continuing until the new line merges into the original stitching line. Come as close as possible to the hipline mark made in Step 3 while maintaining the original contour of the pattern's stitching line. For a dress, extend the new stitching line above the waistline, tapering it into the dart or armhole seam.

5. Mark and trim a new cutting edge ⅝ inch outside the new stitching line.

6. Repeat on the back section of your pattern.

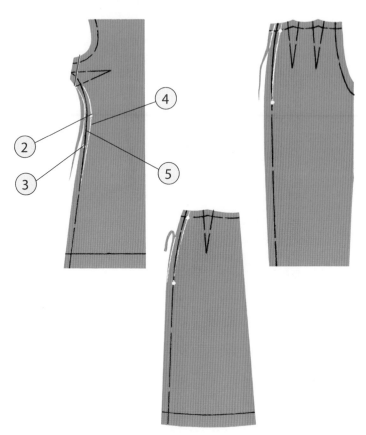

Reducing at the Hipline

1. For a one-piece dress, a skirt or pants, compare your hip measurement *(pages 43–44)* with that printed on the pattern envelope. If your measurement is less than specified, reduce the pattern at the hips.

2. Working on the front section of your pattern, measure in and mark as shown *(white)* ¼ of the amount to be reduced on each side seam.

3. Mark as shown *(white)* the location of your waistline.

4. Draw a new tapered stitching line from the waistline marking made in Step 3 to the new hipline marking made in Step 2; then continue in a line parallel to the original stitching line down to the bottom of the pattern piece.

5. Mark and trim a new cutting edge ⅝ inch outside the new stitching line.

6. Repeat on the back section of your pattern.

Chapter 2: WORKING WITH PATTERNS

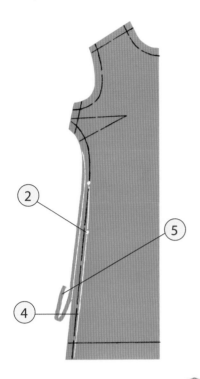

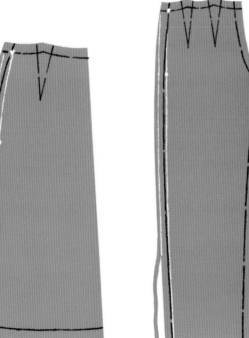

PREPARING TO SEW

Find a flat, firm cutting surface large enough to hold the entire length of your fabric—a table or even the floor, if necessary—and spread out the material as shown at right. Pin and cut out the entire pattern without moving the fabric. To protect your cutting surface, use table pads or a dressmaker's cutting board.

Check the guide sheet that comes with your pattern; it will give several cutting guides—that is, diagrams showing how to arrange the pattern on the material according to its size and the width of the material.

If you are working with striped or checked fabric, use the numbered notches on your pattern pieces (*page 62*) to match the design at important seams. In matching, give priority where possible to front seams over back ones and to horizontal seams over vertical ones.

After cutting out your garment, transfer all pattern markings to the wrong side of the fabric before you remove the pattern. Use a tracing wheel (*page 63*) and dressmaker's carbon paper to do this job quickly and accurately.

Pinning the Pattern to a Solid Fabric

1. Separate all pattern pieces having a line marked "place on fold" and place them on the fabric so that the mark aligns with the fold of the fabric. Pin these pieces to the fabric along the fold.

2. Loosely arrange the other pieces according to the pattern cutting guide, with the printed grain-line arrows parallel to the fold and selvage edges.

3. Measure from the fabric edge to both ends of the grain-line arrow on each pattern piece; make sure that the arrow is uniformly distant from the edge and therefore parallel to it.

4. Smooth each pattern piece to make sure it lies flat. Then pin each piece to the fabric, placing the pins diagonally at the corners and parallel to, and just inside, the cutting line.

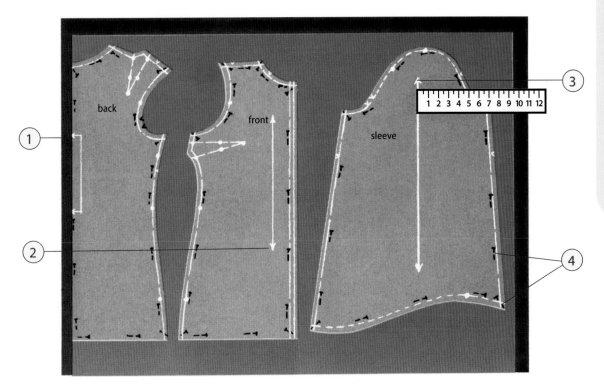

Chapter 2: WORKING WITH PATTERNS

Pinning the Pattern to Striped or Checked Fabric

1. Loosely arrange the pattern pieces on the fabric according to the directions in the pattern layout guide. To make the design match where pieces must be seamed together, look for numbered notches on the patterns for those pieces; make sure that notches having the same numbers lie in exactly the same position relative to the checks or stripes.

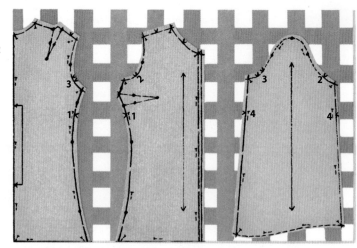

2a. To match design along the most important seam lines of a dress, blouse or shirt, line up notches in the following order: side seams (notches marked 1 in this diagram), armhole and sleeve seams (notches 2 and 3), underarm sleeve seams (notch 4).

2b. To match seam lines of a skirt, line up the side seams (notches marked 1 in this drawing). The center front seam will match because both halves are cut out at once. If the waistband is cut parallel to the grain of the fabric, as in this example, line up the waistband with the waistline edge at the front (notch 2) and then the back (notch 3).

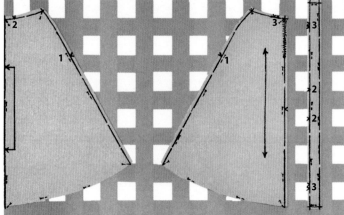

2c. To match seam lines of pants, line up the side seams (notches marked 1 in this drawing) and the inner leg seams (notch 2). If the waistband is cut on the bias, as in this example, the waistband is not matched to the waistline edge.

3. Pin at the notches.

4. Check to be sure that the grain line is parallel to the selvage, or lengthwise edge of the fabric, as in Step 3, and adjust where necessary.

5. Pin the entire pattern to the fabric, as in Step 4.

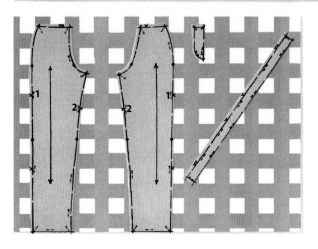

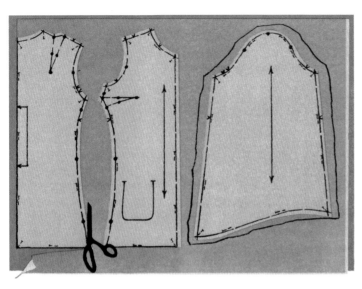

1. Hold the pattern and fabric flat with one hand and cut both together along the printed cutting line with dressmaker's shears. Do not cut out the notches.

2. Before cutting out pattern pieces calling for side or fly-front zippers, see page 105, and page 112.

3. For pattern pieces that are awkward to reach, cut loosely around the entire section, remove it and trim it separately at the cutting line.

Since fabric is flat and the human body is not, the paper patterns that are used as a guide for cutting and sewing garments include numerous instructions—some of them in the form of symbols—to help you convert a two-dimensional fabric into three-dimensional clothing.

For example, the grain line and fold line (*glossary below*) tell how to align the pattern piece with the weave so that the fabric curves properly. Other symbols guide such steps as the joining of two pieces to conform to general body contours (*numbered notches*) and the seaming of individual pieces to fit around pronounced curves such as the bust or buttocks (*broken lines*).

Pattern Markings and Symbols

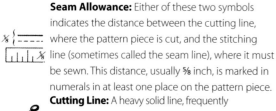

Grain Line: This arrow indicates how to align the pattern piece with the threads of the fabric. Place the line between the arrows, as specified on the pattern piece, on either the lengthwise or the crosswise grain of the fabric—the thread that runs parallel to or at right angles to the finished edge (the selvage) of the fabric.

Fold Line: Either of these two symbols indicates how the edge of the pattern piece aligns with the fabric fold: the bold line of the arrow should line up with the fold.

Seam Allowance: Either of these two symbols indicates the distance between the cutting line, where the pattern piece is cut, and the stitching line (sometimes called the seam line), where it must be sewn. This distance, usually 5/8 inch, is marked in numerals in at least one place on the pattern piece.

Cutting Line: A heavy solid line, frequently accompanied by a drawing of scissors, marks the exact line along which the pattern piece must be cut.

Stitching Line: A thin broken line, frequently accompanied by a drawing of a sewing machine presser foot, marks the exact line along which seams, darts and other construction areas must be stitched. An arrow along the stitching line, or seam line, shows the direction in which the seam must be sewn.

Adjustment Line: A heavy double line indicates the points on the pattern piece at which it may be shortened or lengthened. To lengthen the piece, cut the pattern between the printed lines and add paper. To shorten, pin the pattern up between the double lines.

Notches: These symbols, which are used alone, in pairs or in threes, are always numbered. They mark the exact points along the outer seam lines where sections are joined together; the single notches are joined to single notches, No. 8 notches to No. 8 notches, etc.

Construction Symbols: Large dots, squares and triangles guide construction of a garment—indicating the center front of a sleeve, for example, or marking the point where pieces such as collars and neckline facings must be attached to the garment body. Small dots guide alignment of seams.

Fabric Layout Symbols: A black star indicates that the fabric must be laid out in one thickness, wrong side down, and a single piece of fabric cut. The shaded bar indicates that the pattern piece shaded in the pattern cutting layout is to be placed on the fabric with its printed side down. The other three construction symbols—the large asterisk, dagger and double dagger—are keys to special cutting directions in the pattern instruction sheet.

Button Marking: The horizontal line on this symbol shows exactly where the buttonhole is to be placed and its length is the buttonhole length. The button drawing is the size of the button to be used (the pattern envelope also specifies button sizes).

Zipper Marking: This symbol on the pattern marks the position of the zipper on the garment, and the symbol length is the exact opening length. The top of the slider tab indictates the top of the zipper opening, and the bottom stop, the bottom of the opening.

Preparing to Mark Two Layers of Fabric

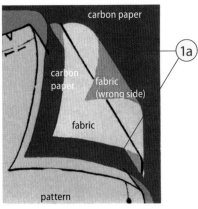

1a. After the pattern has been pinned to the fabric and the fabric pieces have been cut, remove just enough pins, from one piece at a time, so you can slip dressmaker's carbon paper between the layers of fabric and the pattern. Place one piece of carbon paper—carbon side up—under the bottom layer of fabric. Then place another piece of carbon paper—carbon side down—over the top layer of fabric. Pin the pattern back into position.

Preparing to Mark One Layer of Fabric

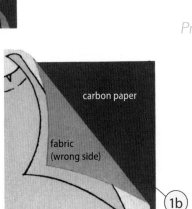

1b. Place one piece of carbon paper—carbon side up—underneath the fabric.

Marking the Fabric

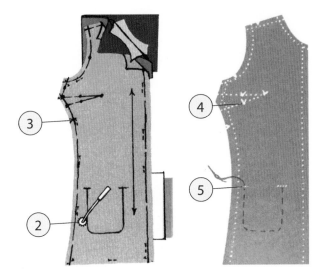

2. Run your tracing wheel along all stitching lines and dart lines. Use a plain (not sawtooth) wheel for knits and doubleknits. Use a straightedge ruler as a guide for straight lines and trace curves freehand. Never reverse the wheel; run it firmly forward.

3. Trace the notches with a dull pencil.

4. With the pencil, draw an X through the center of all circles and dots.

5. Remove the pattern from the fabric and baste along those markings that must show on both sides of the fabric: the center front line and the placement lines for pleats, buttonholes, pockets and trimmings.

Chapter 2: WORKING WITH PATTERNS

ASSEMBLING FIVE
CLASSIC GARMENTS

3

Before immersing yourself in the specific construction details of a garment—its darts, zippers, pleats, pockets, etc., as shown on pages 86 to 171—it will help to get an overall picture of the order in which to tackle these details and consequently to assemble a dress, shirt or blouse, skirt and pants. You can generalize the assembly sequence for these five classic garments to most patterns you will choose to sew.

The assembling procedure is always a logical one: the body section of a blouse, for example, is fitted and sewn before the sleeve is attached, otherwise the armhole in which the sleeve is inserted might not have the proper dimensions. Similarly, buttonholes and buttons are positioned after the garment is otherwise completed, so the closures will be smooth and neat.

If you have chosen the right size pattern (*pages 42–45*) and adjusted it where necessary to your figure (*pages 46–57*), you should encounter very few fitting problems in assembling your garment. But even a perfectly proportioned figure might have some minor quirks: a protruding collarbone that makes a lower neckline desirable, for example, or a slight swayback that necessitates adjusting a waistband. By making such minor fitting adjustments at the points recommended on the following pages, you will ensure that your finished garment hangs properly and fits perfectly.

THE CLASSIC DRESS

Although their styling varies from year to year and season to season, dresses are perhaps the most flattering garment a woman can wear. They skim the body, creating long, fluid lines and gliding over any imperfections. Dresses can be designed to highlight a woman's best features—a short hem draws attention to the legs, a sweetheart neckline emphasizes the face and short sleeves draw attention to arms. A well-fitted dress in a classic design is also timeless and comfortable, and can often be accessorized for day and evening wear.

Basting the Darts and Seams

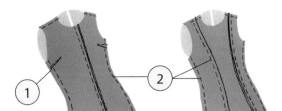

1. Baste the darts, if any.

2. Baste the seams.

3. Turn the dress right side out and try it on.

Adjusting the Darts and the Seams

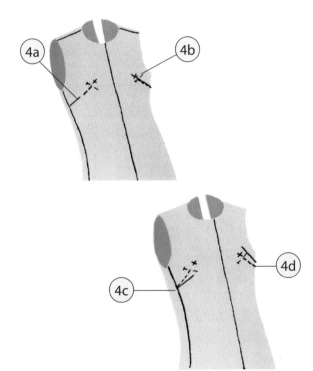

4a. If the bust dart *(solid line)* is too short, it will pucker at the point of the dart when the dress is put on and there will be excess fabric at the fullest part of the bust. To correct it, place a pin 1½ inches from the fullest part of the bust, indicated by an "x" on the drawing. Turn the garment wrong side out and taper *(dotted line)* the dart to the pin. Re-baste the dart.

4b. If the dart *(solid line)* is too long, it will be tight at the fullest part of the bust and pucker at the point of the dart when the dress is tried on. To correct it, place a pin 1½ inches from the fullest part of the bust, indicated by an "x" on the drawing. Turn the garment wrong side out and taper *(dotted line)* the dart to the pin. Re-baste and remove the original basting.

4c. If the bust dart *(solid line)* points below the fullest part of the bust, indicated by an "x," place a pin 1½ inches from the fullest part. Open the dart and draw new stitching lines with chalk from the pin to the original wide ends of the dart; keep the length of the new lines identical to each other. Re-baste.

4d. If the bust dart *(solid line)* points above the fullest part of the bust, as indicated by an "x," place a pin 1½ inches from the fullest part. Open the dart and draw new stitching lines with chalk from the pin to the original wide ends of the dart; keep the length of the new lines identical to each other. Re-baste the dart.

THE CLASSIC DRESS

5a. On dresses with princess seams, if the seams are too tight at the bust, place a pin at the fullest point of the bust, indicated by an "x." Then place pins above and below it where the tightness begins and ends. Let out the desired amount at the center pin and taper above and below it. Baste the new stitching line *(dotted line)*; remove the old basting.

5b. If the princess seam is not snug enough in the midriff, pin the excess fabric together the desired amount, turn the dress wrong side out and baste a new stitching line *(dotted line)*. Remove the old basting line.

5c. Machine stitch the darts and seams. Trim and press open.

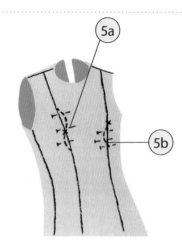

Adjusting the Neckline

6. Baste the back zipper, if any, to the garment and try it on. Close the zipper or pin closed the side or front closures.

7. If the neckline is too tight or too high in the front or back of the garment—remembering to allow for the seam allowance—mark a new stitching line (using pins or chalk) the desired amount below the old stitching line. Trim the seam allowance to ⅝ inch above the new stitching line.

8. Make corresponding changes on the neckline facings.

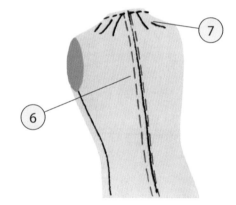

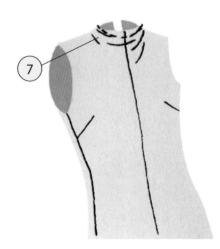

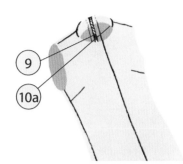

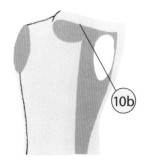

9. Insert the zipper, if any; press.

10a. Attach the neckline facing to the dress; press.

10b. Attach the neckline and center front facings to front closure; press.

Armholes and Sleeves

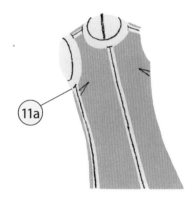

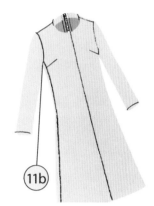

11a. On a sleeveless garment, attach the armhole facings to the garment; press.

11b. On a garment with sleeves, stitch the sleeve seams; press. Then attach the sleeves to the armhole of the dress.

Finishing Touches

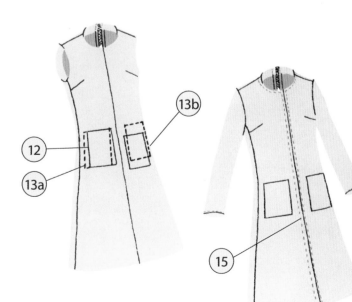

12. Baste the finished patch pockets, if any, to the garment; the average distance is 3½ inches below the natural waistline. Try on for position.

13a. If the pockets seem to crowd the front of the dress *(solid line)*, move them to the side *(dotted line)*.

13b. If the pockets are so low *(solid line)* that you have to bend at the waist to reach the pocket bottom, reposition them *(dotted line)*.

14. Stitch the pocket to the garment; press.

15. Add a decorative line of machine topstitching along the edges and seam lines if desired.

16. Try on the dress and mark the sleeve and skirt lengths; hem and press.

THE CLASSIC SHIRT

A classically styled, carefully fitted shirt is a staple of a man's wardrobe, as well as a fundamental building block for many other garments. Coats, jackets and even some women's dresses are simply variations on a tailored shirt. Learning to make this one garment can unlock your ability to make many others.

The Body Section

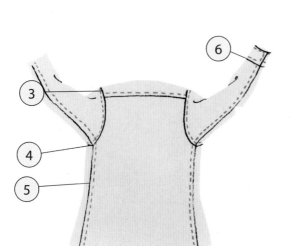

1. Sew the yoke pieces, if any, to the shirt back and front. Topstitch if desired.

2. Join the shirt front to the back at the shoulders if there is no yoke.

Sleeves and Side Seams

3. Make the sleeve placket and attach the sleeve to the body section of the shirt; press.

4. Construct flat felled seams around the armhole of the shirt.

5. Sew up the underarm and side seams of the shirt.

6. Attach the cuffs to the sleeves and topstitch if desired.

THE CLASSIC SHIRT

Collars and Facings

7. Fold back the facing at the front opening or attach the placket. Topstitch the placket if desired.

8. Attach the collar to the shirt.

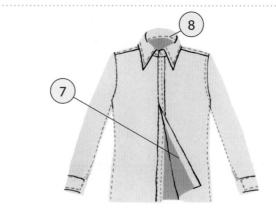

Buttonholes and Buttons

9. Mark the buttonholes on the shirt body and cuffs.

10. Try on the shirt and pin it closed at the buttonhole markings.

11. If the fabric gaps at the buttonhole markings or bunches up in between, remove the pins and reposition them.

12. When the shirt closes smoothly and evenly, make the buttonholes and sew on the buttons.

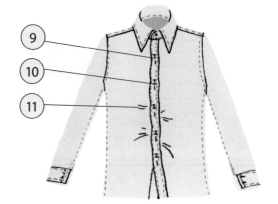

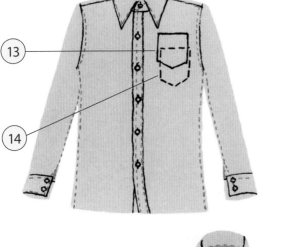
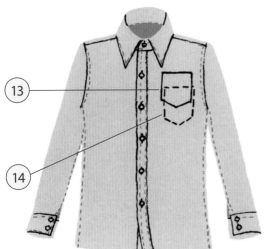

13. Baste the finished breast pocket or pockets to the shirt and try the shirt on for positioning.

14. If the pocket is so high that it comes close to the tip of the collar, and is uncomfortable to reach, reposition it *(dotted lines)* on the shirt.

15. Sew the pocket to the shirt; press.

Finishing Touches

16. Try on the shirt and mark its length; hem and press.

THE CLASSIC BLOUSE

A blouse is different from a shirt in that it is slimmer, yet shaped to a woman's more rounded body. Like a shirt, however, the blouse is also the basis for a number of other garments, especially dresses. As with so many women's clothes, the effect of a blouse depends on the fabric you choose for it. The same pattern will look vastly different made in shimmery silk, crisp cotton or lightweight flannel, yet should fit and flatter regardless of the fabric.

Body Section

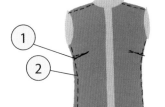

1. Baste the darts, if any.

2. Baste the seams.

3. Try on the blouse and adjust the darts and seams if necessary *(The Classic Dress, Steps 4A–5C, pages 67–68)*.

4. Stitch the darts and seams; press.

Facings and Collars

5. Attach the facing or fold back the self-facing at the center front opening; press.

6. Attach the collar to the neckline of the blouse; press.

Sleeves

7. Make the sleeve and cuff; press.

8. Attach the sleeve to the armhole of the blouse.

Finishing Touches

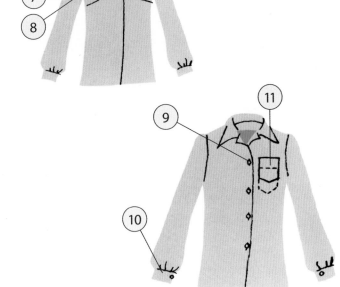

9. Mark the buttonholes and try on the blouse for positioning *(The Classic Shirt, Steps 9–12, page 72)*.

10. Sew the buttons on the blouse and cuff.

11. Baste the finished breast pocket to the blouse and check its position *(The Classic Shirt, Steps 13–15, page 73)*.

12. Try on the blouse for length; hem and press.

THE CLASSIC SKIRT

Skirts can be long or short, full or slim, and made of sturdy or lightweight fabric. There are so many variations, and many women consider skirts viable, flattering and comfortable alternatives to pants. Despite the many design alternatives, most skirts are quite similar in their construction and one of the simplest garments to master.

Darts and Seams on Pleated Skirts

1. Fold and baste the pleats, if any, in place.

2. Baste the darts and seams of the pleated skirt and try it on.

3. If the pleat gapes or rolls open *(solid lines)*, remove the basting at the waistline and lift the underlay of the pleat until it falls properly *(dotted lines)*. Re-baste.

4. Stitch the darts, seams and pleats in place; press.

Darts and Seams on Unpleated Skirts

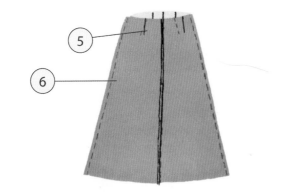

5. Baste the darts, if any.

6. Baste the seams.

7. Try on the skirt.

8a. If the dart points away from the fullest part of the hip or abdomen, indicated by an "x", place a pin 1½ inches above the fullest part of the protrusion. Remove the dart bastings and draw new stitching lines from the pin, marking the new tip of the dart to the original wide ends of the dart; the lines must be the same length. Re-baste the dart.

8b. If the waist dart is too short *(solid line)*, it will pucker at the tip when tried on and the skirt will have excess fabric at the hip or abdomen. Correct it by placing a pin 1½ inches above the fullest part of the upper hip or abdomen, indicated by an "x" on the drawing, and tapering the dart to the pin. Re-baste the dart.

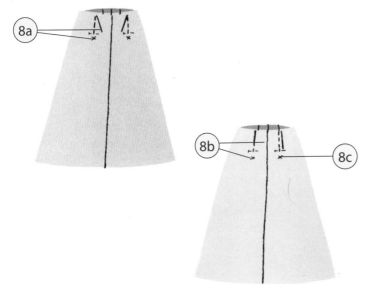

8c. If the dart is too long, the skirt will be tight over the upper hip or abdomen and the dart will pucker at the tip when tried on. Correct it by placing a pin 1½ inches above the fullest part of the protrusion, indicated by an "x" on the drawing, tapering the dart to the pin, and re-basting.

9. Sew all darts and seams; press.

THE CLASSIC SKIRT

Zipper and Waistband

10. Baste the zipper, if any, to the skirt.

11. Baste the waistband or waistline facing to the skirt.

12. Try on the skirt.

13. If the skirt below the waistband bulges because the band is too high on the back, mark a new stitching line with pins or chalk to the desired width. Remove the waistband; trim the skirt seam allowance to ⅝ inch above the new stitching line.

14. Insert the zipper, if any, to the skirt.

15. Attach the waistband or waistline facing to the skirt.

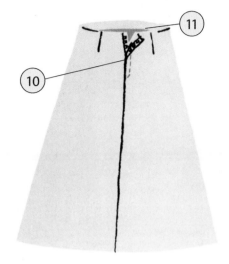

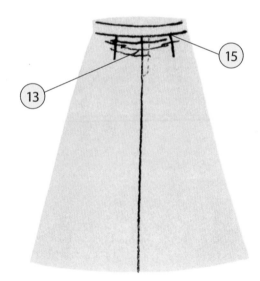

Front Closures

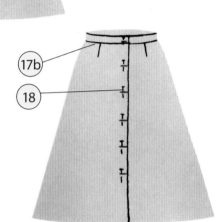

16. Turn back the center front facings, if any.

17a. Stitch the waistline facing to the skirt.

17b. Stitch the waistband to the skirt.

18. Mark the buttonhole positions.

19. Try on the skirt and pin closed at the buttonhole markings. Move the pins if necessary to adjust the closure.

20. Make the buttonholes and sew on the buttons and hooks and eyes or snaps, if any.

Finishing Touches

21. Baste the finished patch pockets, if any, to the skirt and try on for position (*The Classic Dress, Steps 12 and 13, page 69*).

22. Stitch the pockets to the skirt; press.

23. Try on the skirt and mark its length; hem and press.

The search for the perfect pair of pants ends once you have perfectly fitted a pants pattern. By your choice of fabric you can create endless variations, ranging from jeans to trousers and flowing evening pants. You can change the look by moving the zipper from front to side or even back. And following fashion's dictates is as easy as changing the hemline or redrawing the leg width from wide to narrow—or back again.

Darts, Seams and Zippers

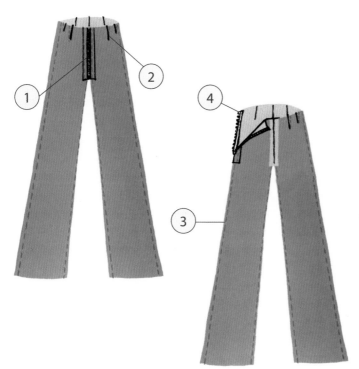

1. If you are inserting a fly-front zipper, mark the length of the zipper opening and reinforce the crotch at the bottom.

2. Baste the darts, if any, and try on to adjust the fit if necessary *(The Classic Skirt, Step 8, page 77)*. Stitch the darts.

3. Baste and stitch the outer pants leg to the bottom of the in-seam side pocket, if any. Insert the pocket, then baste and stitch the inner-leg seams and crotch seam.

4. Insert the side, back or fly-front zipper.

THE CLASSIC WOMEN'S PANTS

Waistband or Waistline Facing

5a. If you are making pants without a waistband, baste the facing to the waistline.

5b. If you are making pants with a waistband, baste it to the pants.

6. Try on the pants and adjust the waistband or facing if necessary, *(The Classic Skirt, Step 13, page 78)*.

7. Stitch the waistband, if any, to the pants; press.

8. Make buttonholes and sew on buttons, snaps or hooks and eyes, if any.

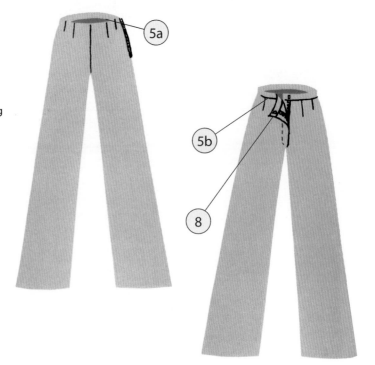

9. Baste the finished patch pockets, if any, to the pants. Try on and adjust the position *(The Classic Dress, Steps 12 and 13, page 69)*, then stitch; press.

10. Try on the pants and mark the length; hem and press.

With its simple lines and proportions, the basic pants pattern will help you make most men's trousers, casual pants, jeans, and even shorts. Because men have fewer curves than women, they are generally easier to fit and their fashions are more forgiving. Master the front fly and side pockets, and you will be able to confidently make a variety of pants to suit any occasion.

Zipper and Seams

1. Insert the fly-front zipper.

2. Baste and stitch the outer-leg seams to the bottom of the in-seam side pocket, if any, then insert the pocket. Baste and stitch the inner-leg seams and crotch seam; press.

Waistband

3. Attach the waistband to the pants; press.

4. Make buttonholes or attach snaps or hooks and eyes to the belt.

Finishing Touches

5. Baste the finished patch pockets, if any, to the pants. Try on and adjust the position if necessary *(The Classic Dress, Steps 12 and 13, page 69)* and stitch; press.

6. Try on the pants and mark the length; hem and press.

DETAILS OF GARMENT CONSTRUCTION

Now that you know the construction sequence for your project, it's time to review the instructions for assembling specific elements of your garment—the seams, pockets, zippers, sleeves, etc. As you follow the workflow suggested on pages 64 to 85, return to these step-by-step instructions to complete each phase of assembly.

These instructions are no doubt more detailed and demanding than those you are used to seeing, or those you found in your pattern envelope. They will take longer to complete. However, the result will be a perfectly fitted, soundly constructed, custom-tailored garment that will last for years and stand as a testimony to your sewing skill.

SEAMS

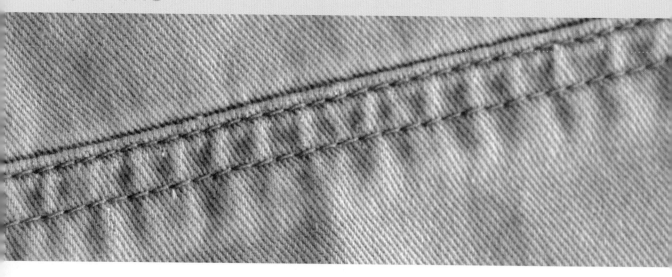

Seams not only hold pieces of a garment together—they are also the most obvious indicators of whether a garment is well or poorly made. With the techniques shown here, you can sew as flat, smooth and finished-looking a seam as any professional dressmaker might make.

There are various problems involved in making a basic "plain seam": getting two seams to intersect properly, "easing" a longer piece of fabric into the seam line of a smaller piece, working on curves, reducing bulkiness and finishing the raw edges. All of these are encountered as well in making other, more complicated types of seams, such as the strong seam used on men's shirts that is known as a flat felled seam—a double seam in which the raw edges of the seam are folded over and encased inside a second row of stitching.

Essential to the success of all seams is careful marking and basting, followed by machine stitching with the proper needle, thread and stitch size for your fabric and garment. Even more important is a smooth pressing of each seam as soon as it is completed; not even the most thorough pressing of the finished garment can substitute for pressing each seam as you go.

Basting and Stitching the Plain Seam

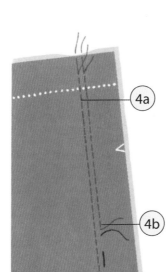

1. With the wrong sides of the fabric facing outward, pin together the pieces to be seamed, inserting the pins at right angles to the stitching line *(white)*. Match and pin first where the seam-line markings intersect.

2. Match and pin next at the notch markings; add more pins at 1- to 2-inch intervals on a straight seam and at intervals as short as ¼ inch on a curved seam.

3. Baste *(red)* just outside the seam-line markings and remove pins.

4a. After trying on the garment for fit, machine stitch *(blue)* directly along the seam-line markings; remove the bastings.

4b. An added step for knit fabrics: to reinforce the seams, machine stitch a second line ⅛ inch outside the first seam.

5. Press open.

wrong side

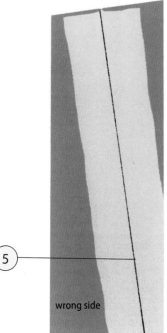
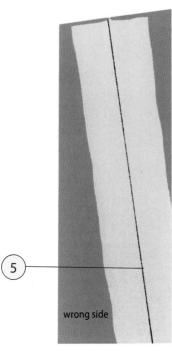

wrong side

SEAMS: THE PLAIN SEAM

Finishing Seam Edges

6a. For a simple finish on tightly woven fabrics, trim the seam allowance to ½ inch, using dressmaker's shears.

6b. For a more decorative cut edge on a tightly woven fabric, use pinking shears.

6c. For a simple finish on moderately ravelly knit and woven fabrics, machine stitch ½ inch from the seam, then trim with dressmaker's shears—or for a more decorative cut edge on woven fabrics, use pinking shears. Make sure you do not cut into the machine stitching.

6d. For ravelly knit and woven fabrics, use a zigzag attachment to machine stitch a line ½ inch from the seam. Then trim away the excess seam allowance close to the zigzag stitching, making sure you do not snip into it.

6e. To hand finish ravelly fabrics, trim the seam allowance to make it even, then sew *(black)* with an overcast stitch *(page 27)*.

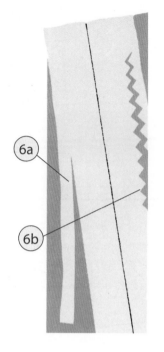

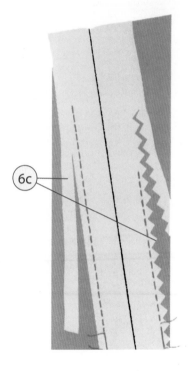

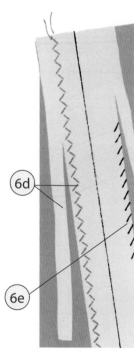

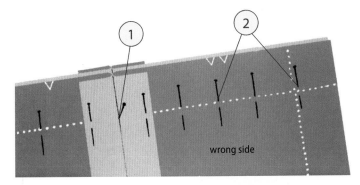

wrong side

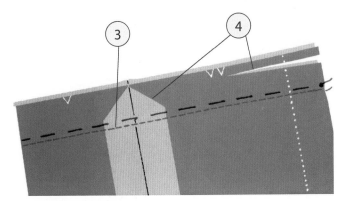

1. To be sure that stitched seams on two sections of a garment will intersect accurately when joined together, match the two sections with wrong sides facing outward. Insert a pin at the point where the new stitching line crosses the stitched seams; bring the pin up at right angles to the new stitching line.

2. Match and pin at each end where the seam markings *(white)* intersect and at the notch markings; add more pins at 1- to 2-inch intervals on a straight seam and at intervals as short as ¼ inch on a curved seam, making sure that all seam allowances are pinned flat.

3. Baste *(red)* and machine stitch *(blue)* as for a plain seam.

4. Trim to ½ inch and diagonally clip the four corners of the joined seam allowances.

1. Run a line of basting *(red)* ⅛ inch outside the stitching line *(white)* on the longer piece of fabric, sewing between the pattern markings that indicate the area to be eased. Use a short basting stitch—six stitches per inch—and leave 4 inches of loose thread at both ends (use thread the color of your final stitching—this basting will remain inside the finished seam to help keep it flat).

2. Pin the seam together between the ends of the seam and the ease markings, leaving open the area to be eased.

3. Wrap the loose end of the ease-line basting thread around the pin marking one end of the area to be eased.

4. Pull the loose thread at the other end until the longer seam is as short as the shorter seam, then wrap the thread around the pin at that end.

5. Distribute the excess fabric evenly between the ease markings and pin.

6. Baste and machine stitch *(blue)* the entire length of the seam.

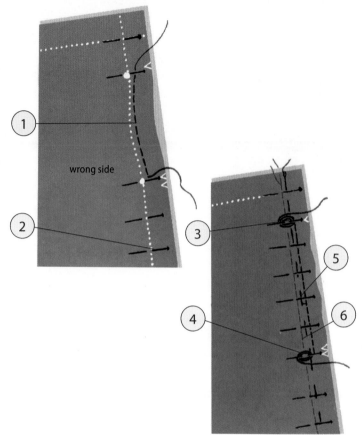

wrong side

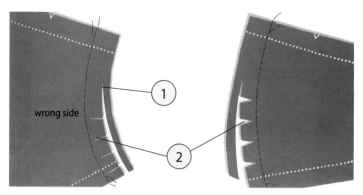

1. After machine stitching *(blue)* a concave or convex seam (using a stitch slightly smaller than usual because of the curve), trim the seam allowance to ½ inch.

2. Clip (for concave) or notch (for convex) at ¼- to ½-inch intervals (the sharper the curve, the shorter the intervals), cutting to within ⅛ inch of the machine stitching. Press open.

SEAMS: THE FLAT FELLED SEAM

Preparing to Make the Flat Felled Seam

1. Make a plain seam, as shown in Steps 1–4, page 89, with either the right sides—the sides that will be visible in the completed garment—or the wrong sides of the fabric together, depending on your pattern. Press the seam open. Then fold and press both seam allowances in the direction indicated on your pattern.

2. Trim the underneath seam allowance to ⅛ inch.

3. Trim the top seam allowance to ½ inch.

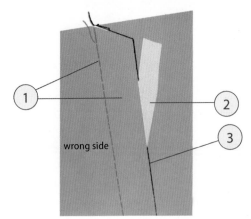

wrong side

Folding the Flat Felled Seam

4. Fold the top seam allowance over the underneath one, lining up the edge of the top seam allowance along the machine stitching *(blue)* of the original plain seam; this encloses the underneath seam allowance.

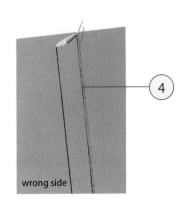

wrong side

Basting and Stitching the Flat Felled Seam

5. Turn the fold to the side on which the felled seam should fall.

6. Pin the felled seam, inserting the pins from the folded edge toward the seam at right angles.

7. Baste *(red)* ⅛ inch from the folded edge.

8. Machine stitch midway between the basting and the folded edge. Remove the basting and press.

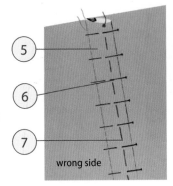

wrong side

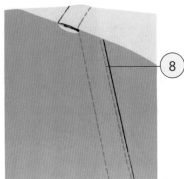

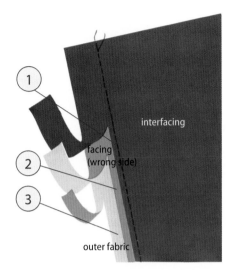

interfacing

facing
(wrong side)

outer fabric

1. To reduce the bulk of seam allowances where there is a facing (a layer of fabric backing at garment edges) and an interfacing (a stiff fabric, shown here in dark gray, between the outside of the garment and the facing), trim the seam allowance of the interfacing to 1/16 of inch.

2. Trim the seam allowance of the facing to 1/8 inch.

3. Trim the seam allowance of the outer fabric to 1/4 inch.

4. To reduce seam bulk at corners that have been faced and perhaps also interfaced, trim both sides of the corner, starting 1½ inches from the corner on the outer fabric and cutting through all layers. Do not cut closer to the stitching line than 1/16 inch.

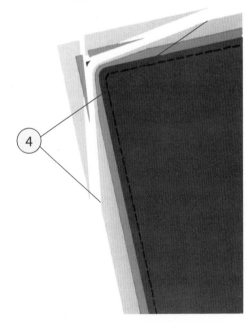

DARTS

Darts, those stitched tapered folds that help to shape flat pieces of fabric to the curves and bumps of the human body, can also be used decoratively: their placement and manner of stitching often add to the design of a garment.

There are really only two kinds of darts, and both are based on triangular shapes. The most common type begins with the wide part of the fold at a seam and narrows to a point. This is the single-pointed dart and is placed at waist, bust, elbow or shoulder seams. The vertical double-pointed dart is less common; it is used to give contour to a waistless dress or long blouse or jacket.

As simple as darts are, making them look smoothly perfect requires careful adjustment to the pattern and precise marking, stitching and pressing. You will find that it is worth the few extra minutes needed to make the extra markings recommended on page 97, which prevent an off-center or misplaced dart; in addition, a seemingly small step—sewing a few stitches off the fabric edge at the dart tip—can eliminate a puckered point.

Getting Ready to Make Darts

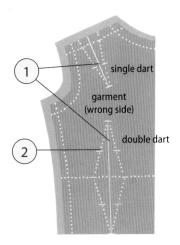

1. In addition to the pattern markings traced *(dotted lines)* on the wrong side of the fabric, draw in a vertical tine *(white)* marking the center of the darts where they will be folded.

2. Place short horizontal markings *(white)* at the tips and at the widest parts of the darts, and at the midway points between the two.

single dart

garment
(wrong side)

double dart

Pinning the Darts

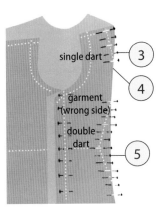

3. Fold back the body section along the center line of each dart, matching the horizontal markings.

4. Pin the single dart first at the seam line, next at the tip and then at the midpoint. Add intervening pins at 1-inch intervals.

5. Pin the double dart first at the widest point, next at the tips and then at the midpoints. Add intervening pins at 1-inch intervals.

single dart

garment
(wrong side)

double
dart

Basting and Fitting

6. Baste *(red)* just inside the stitching line, securing the thread with a fastening stitch *(page 28)* at both ends.

7. Baste the seams of the garment together just outside the stitching line. Try on and adjust the garment for fit.

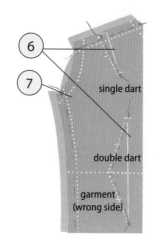

single dart

double dart

garment
(wrong side)

Finishing the Single Dart

8. Remove only enough of the seam basting around the dart to permit you to stitch the dart.

9. Machine stitch *(blue)*, beginning at the widest end.

10. Sew a few stitches off the edge of the fabric at the tip end. Then cut the thread and hand knot. Remove the dart bastings.

11a. Press average-sized darts on medium-weight fabric so that the fold is toward the center of the garment, except for the bust dart, which is pressed down.

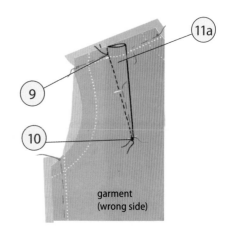

garment
(wrong side)

11b. On very wide darts or heavy fabrics, cut along the center fold line to within 1 inch of the tip, and trim seams to ⅝ inch; press the dart open as shown. Press the tip toward the center.

Finishing the Double Dart

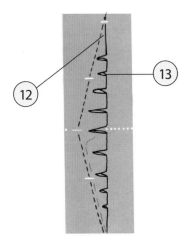

12. Machine stitch, beginning at one tip, at the very edge of the fold; sew a few stitches off the fabric edge at the other tip, then cut the thread and hand knot the threads at both tips *(page 19)*. Remove bastings.

13. Clip into the dart at 1-inch intervals to within ⅛ inch of the stitching line.

14. Press toward the center of the garment.

PLEATS

The only secret to making a perfect pleat is to take the time to mark and fold it absolutely accurately—a small price to pay for the grace, movement and controlled fullness pleats can add to a garment.

The classic pleat is a straight pleat. It can be used singly or in a series in which each pleat is folded to lie in the same direction; it can also be used to form an inverted pleat, in which two pleats are turned toward each other to meet in the center. Pleats can be left unpressed, for a soft, draping effect, or firmly pressed along their folds for a crisp, tailored look. For an even more tailored look, pressed pleats can also be stitched on the side of the fabric that will be visible when the garment is completed, from the top edge to a point partway down the pleat.

The actual steps in making a pleat are few and simple. But to ensure evenly spaced, straight pleats, work on a flat surface large enough to lay out the entire piece to be pleated, and keep all basting stitches in until you reach the stage recommended in the instructions opposite.

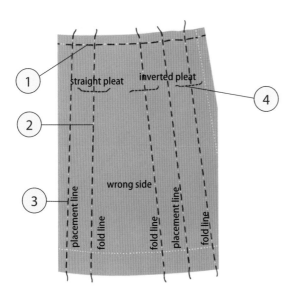

1. Run a line of basting *(green)* along the waistline seam marking *(white)*.

2. Unless you have done so already, run a line of basting following pattern markings for the fold line (the line along which the pleat will be folded).

3. In this case, using a different colored thread, run a line of basting following pattern markings for the placement line (the line against which the folded pleat will be placed).

4. If you plan to press the pleat and topstitch it partway closed, use a horizontal running stitch *(page 21)* to mark the position on the fold line where the topstitching should end.

PLEATS

Constructing the Pleats

5. With the fabric wrong side down, fold each pleat on its fold line and pin it against its placement line. Begin to pin at the bottom to ensure an even hemline, and make sure to catch all layers of fabric. (The number of pleats and the direction in which they are folded will depend upon your pattern.)

6. Baste *(red)* the folded pleats, stitching from the bottom of the garment to the top, ¼ inch from the fold. Stitch through all layers of fabric.

7. Machine stitch *(blue)* along the waistline seam, a fraction above the basted markings, to hold the pleats in place.

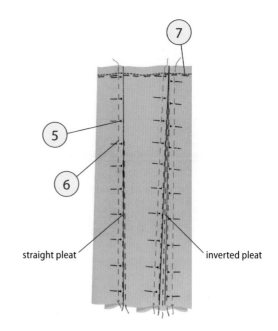

straight pleat   inverted pleat

Finishing the Unpressed Pleat

8a. Remove the bastings after the garment has been assembled and is ready to hem; the pleats will then fall in soft folds from the waistline.

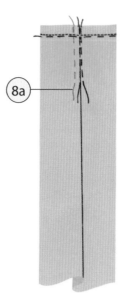

8b. After pressing the pleats on both sides of the fabric and assembling the garment, remove only enough of the bastings to enable you to hem the skirt. Do not remove the remaining pleat bastings, including the placement line, until the garment has been assembled, hemmed and pressed again.

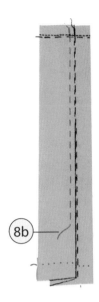

Finishing the Topstitched Pleat

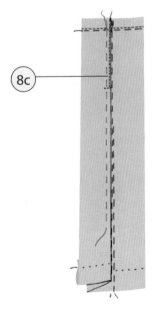

8c. After pressing the pleats and assembling the garment, add a line of machine stitching on the right side of the fabric, the side that will be visible when the garment is completed, ⅛ inch from the edge of the fold of each pleat. Stitch from the waistline down to the horizontal marker made in Step 4 or to the point most becoming to you. Follow the instructions in Step 8b for hemming, removal of bastings and final pressing.

ZIPPERS

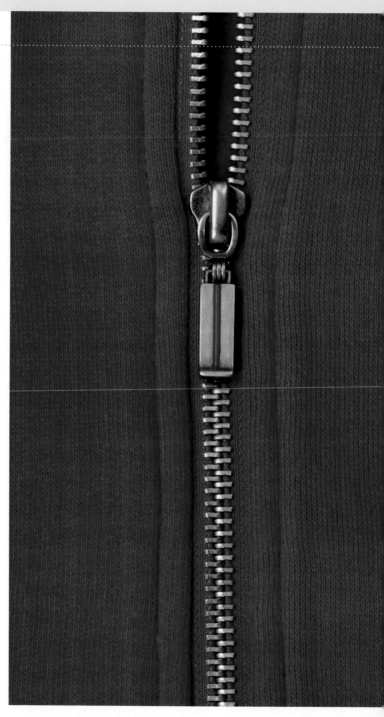

Although zippers have intimidated the home sewer for years, it is perfectly possible to make a neat, smooth zipper without an unsightly gap or bulge.

Resist the temptation to take shortcuts or to insert the zipper before the garment is assembled. Only by fitting the garment and making the necessary adjustments to darts and seams—including the zipper seam—before putting the zipper in will you ensure a perfect fit.

The most common way of inserting a zipper is the centered application, used in neckline and center back and front closings, in which the zipper is concealed under two flaps and has two rows of stitching visible. In the lapped application, used in side seam closings for skirts, women's pants and dresses, the zipper is concealed beneath a single wide lap, with only one line of stitching visible. The fly-front zipper, providing a wide lap of fabric over the zipper, is used on the front of men's and sometimes women's pants.

Select a zipper in the color of your fabric and the length specified on the pattern. One final tip: before inserting the zipper, press it flat.

Preparing the Pants Front

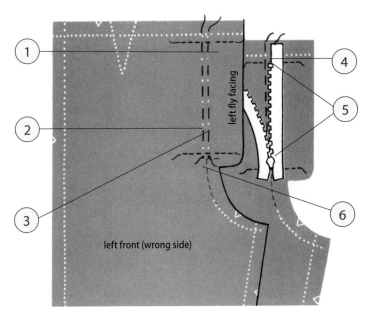

left fly facing

left front (wrong side)

1. If your pattern does not include fly facings as part of the front sections, pin the fly pattern to the front section when laying the pattern on the fabric. Cut as if one piece.

2. Baste *(green)* along the center front seam-line marking *(white)* of the left front section, stitching the length of the fly facing.

3. Run a line of basting parallel to the basted line made in Step 2, and ¼ inch toward the fly facing. This will become the fly fold line.

4. Place the open zipper face down on the left center seam line, so that the zipper's top stop is ¼ inch below the waist seam line.

5. Mark the position of the top and bottom stops with chalk or pins; re-mark with a horizontal running stitch *(page 21)*.

6. To reinforce the crotch, machine stitch *(blue)* a line beginning at the left fly fold line ¼ inch below the marking for the bottom stop. Stitch across from the fold line to the center seam line and then down 1 inch along the center seam line.

7. Repeat Steps 2–6 on the right front pants section.

Assembling the Pants

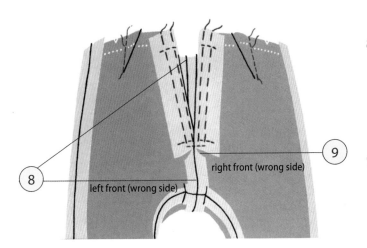

right front (wrong side)

left front (wrong side)

8. To ensure the proper hang of the garment, assemble the pants in the following Sequence: sew and press the darts, the outer leg seams and the inner leg seams. Then join the legs by sewing the center seam, beginning at the center back waistline and ending at the bottom stop marking on the center front seam line.

9. With the tips of a scissors, clip into the center front seam allowance at the base of the fly facing, cutting diagonally to within 1/16 inch of the line of reinforcement stitching made in Step 6.

ZIPPERS: WOMEN'S FLY-FRONT ZIPPER

Sewing the Zipper to the Right Fly Facing

10. Place the right front of the pants wrong side down and extend the right fly facing so that it lies flat.

11. Place the open zipper face down on the extended right fly facing, so that the top stop is on the horizontal marking made in Step 5. The teeth should be flush against the basted fold line. Pin the right zipper tape to the facing.

12. Baste *(red)* the zipper tape to the right fly facing ¼ inch from the outer edge of the tape. Remove the pins.

13. Using a zipper foot, machine stitch ⅛ inch from the teeth. Remove the basting.

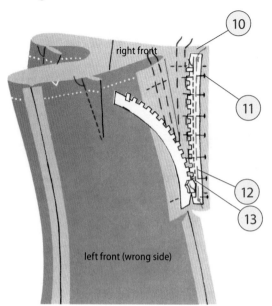

Sewing the Zipper to the Left Front

14. Turn the pants right side out.

15. Fold the left fly facing to the inside along the basted fold line.

16. Pin and baste the loose, unstitched zipper tape, wrong side down, to the left front through all layers—the pants front, fly facing and zipper tape—with the top stop of the zipper at the horizontal marking and the zipper teeth extending just beyond the fold of the fabric. Remove the pins.

17. On the side of the fabric that will be visible in the completed garment, machine stitch the zipper to the left front near the fold. Close the zipper.

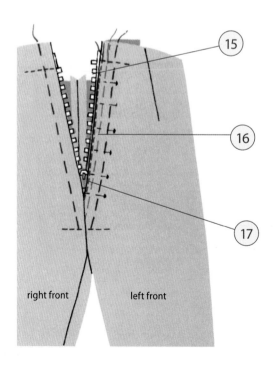

Finishing the Fly Front

18. Lap the right front over the zipper until the fabric lies flat, covers the teeth and meets the center seam line of the left front. Pin in place close to the folded edge.

19. Hand baste the zipper from top to bottom on the right front, staying 1 inch from the folded edge. Baste to within 1 inch of the bottom stop, then curve the basting until it meets the center seam. Remove the pins.

20. Turn the pants wrong side out.

21. Slide the pants wrong side down under the zipper foot and begin stitching at the center seam, just outside the basting. To reinforce the fly, stitch forward two stitches, then back two stitches and then forward the length of the zipper. Remove the basting and press.

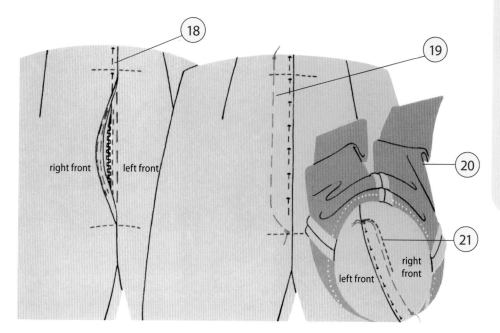

right front   left front

left front   right front

Determining the Length of the Zipper Opening

1. Pin the center back seam *(white)* of the garment closed after the garment has been fitted and all darts and other seams have been sewn and pressed.

2. Place the open zipper face down on the center back seam line so that the zipper's top stop is ¼ inch below the markings for the neck seam line.

3. Mark the position of the top and bottom stops of the zipper on the center back seam line with chalk or a pin. Then re-mark, using a horizontal running stitch *(page 21)*, as indicated in green; extend these marks across the two center back seam allowances.

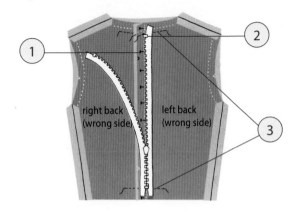

right back (wrong side)   left back (wrong side)

Preparing the Seam

4. Baste *(red)* the center back seam from the bottom of the garment pieces to the marking for the bottom stop; remove the pins. Machine stitch *(blue)* and remove the basting.

5. Baste closed the remainder of the center back seam, stitching on the seam-line marking from the bottom stop to the neck edge.

6. After pressing open the center back seam, lay the garment on the right back and extend the seam allowance of the right back so that it lies flat.

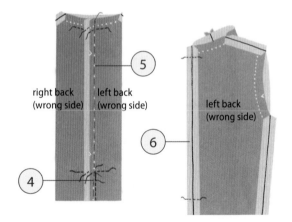

right back (wrong side)   left back (wrong side)

left back (wrong side)

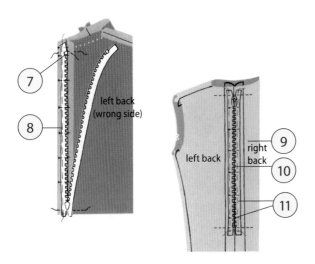

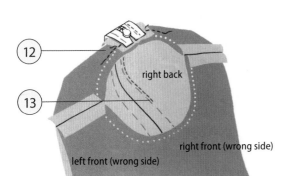

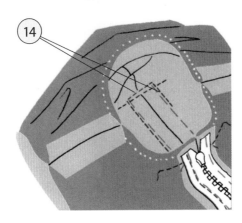

7. Place the open zipper face down on the extended right back seam allowance with the top stop at the horizontal marking made in Step 3 and the teeth flush against the center back seam. Pin the left tape to the back seam allowance.

8. Baste the zipper tape to the extended seam allowance, using short stitches placed ¼ inch from the teeth and remove the pins.

9. Close the zipper and turn the garment right side out.

10. Hold the zipper inside the garment so that it is centered on the seam; pin it across both center back seam allowances.

11. Hand baste along both sides of the zipper ¼ inch from the center seam line, catching all layers—the garment fabric, the seam allowance and the zipper tape. Remove the pins.

Stitching the Zipper

12. Turn the garment wrong side out.

13. Slide the right side of the fabric—the side that will be visible when the garment is completed—into the machine and, using a zipper foot, stitch down the right-hand side of the zipper, just outside the basting line, from the neck edge to ⅛ inch below the bottom stop marking.

14. Continue stitching across and up the left side of the zipper to the neck edge. Snip open the center seam basting, remove all other bastings and press.

Preparing the Side Seam for the Insertion of the Zipper

1. If your pattern does not provide an extra-wide seam allowance of 1 inch for the side zipper, add it to the side seam as you cut out the fabric.

2. With wrong sides facing out, pin closed the left side seam *(white)*, then mark *(green)* the length of the zipper as shown for the centered zipper, page 108, Steps 1–3.

3. Baste *(red)* the side seam from the hemline up to the marking for the bottom stop; remove the pins. Machine stitch *(blue)*, then remove the basting.

4. Baste closed the remainder of the side seam directly on the seam-line marking from the bottom stop to the waistline edge.

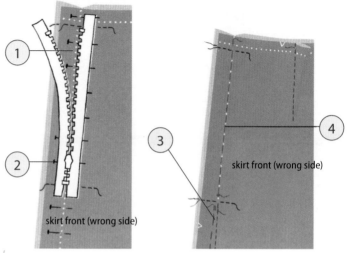

skirt front (wrong side)

skirt front (wrong side)

Sewing the Zipper to the Skirt Back

5. Press open the side seam.

6. Lay the garment down on the back section and extend the back seam allowance so that it lies flat.

7. Place the open zipper face down on the extended back seam allowance, with its top and bottom stops at the horizontal markings made in Step 2. The teeth should be flush against the closed side seam. Pin the left tape to the back seam allowance.

8. Baste the zipper tape to the extended back seam allowance close to the teeth. Work from the bottom of the zipper tape to the top, machine basting with a zipper foot or using short hand stitches. Remove the pins.

9. Close the zipper and fold the back seam allowance under the garment along the line of basting made in Step 8, thus causing the zipper to flip up.

10. Pin together all layers of the fabric—the front seam allowance, the skirt front and back, and the back seam allowance.

11. Using a zipper foot, machine stitch along the narrow strip of folded seam allowance from the bottom of the zipper tape to the top. Remove the pins.

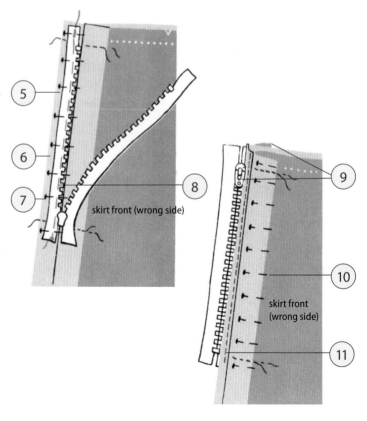

skirt front (wrong side)

skirt front (wrong side)

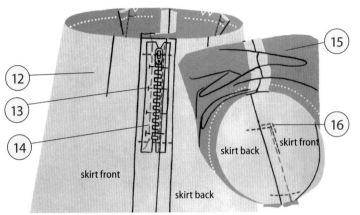

skirt front

skirt back

skirt back

skirt front

12. Turn the skirt right side out.

13. Hold the zipper inside the skirt so that it lies flat on the seam. Pin it in place across both seam allowances.

14. Hand baste ½ inch from the side seam up the skirt front from the bottom stop marking to the top edge, sewing through all layers—the skirt front, front seam allowance and the zipper tape. Remove pins.

15. Turn the skirt wrong side out.

16. Slide the skirt front, wrong side down, under the zipper foot. Beginning at the side seam and following a line ⅛ inch outside the marking for the bottom stop made in Step 2, page 110, stitch across the bottom and up the length of the zipper to the top edge of the garment. Then snip open the side seam basting, remove all other bastings and press.

ZIPPERS: MEN'S FLY-FRONT ZIPPER

Preparing the Pants Front

1. If you have not already done so, run a line of basting *(green)* along the waist seam-line marking *(white)* of each front section so that it will show on both sides of the fabric.

2. On the right pants front, run a line of basting parallel to the center seam line and ¼ inch outside it, extending from the waistline edge to the bottom of the fly opening marked on the pattern; this will become the fly fold line.

3. To reinforce the crotch on each front section, machine stitch *(blue)* along the center seam line, beginning 1 inch below the marking for the bottom of the fly opening and ending 1 inch above that point.

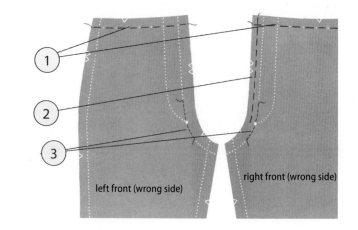

right front (wrong side)

left front (wrong side)

Joining the Pants Front

4. Pin together the pants front pieces along the center seam line.

5. Baste *(red)* along the center seam line at the crotch, then remove the pins. Machine stitch from the mark for the bottom of the fly opening to 1 inch from the inner leg seam line.

Making the Left Fly

6. Pin and baste the interfacing *(dark gray)* to the wrong side of the left fly. Remove the pins, machine stitch, then remove the basting.

7. Trim the seam allowance—of the interfacing only—close to the machine stitching.

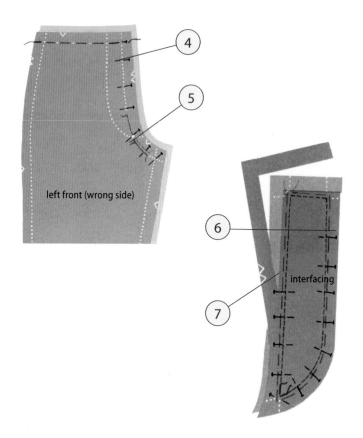

left front (wrong side)

interfacing

Attaching the Left Fly to the Left Pants Front

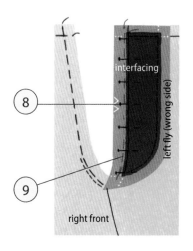

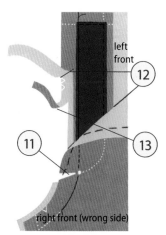

8. With the wrong sides of the fabric facing outward, pin the left fly to the left pants front along the center seam line, making sure that the markings for the seam intersections and notches match.

9. Baste the left fly to the left pants front along the center seam line, starting at the top edge of the pants and ending at the bottom of the fly opening. Remove the pins, machine stitch and remove the bastings.

10. Fold the right pants front over the left pants front.

11. Clip through the center seam allowances at the base of the fly, pushing away the fly fabric itself so that it is not clipped.

12. Trim the center seam allowance of the fly to within ⅛ inch of the machine stitching, from the diagonal clip made in Step 11 to the waistline edge.

13. Trim the center seam allowance of the left pants front to within ¼ inch of the machine stitching, from the diagonal clip to the waistline edge.

Attaching the Zipper to the Left Fly

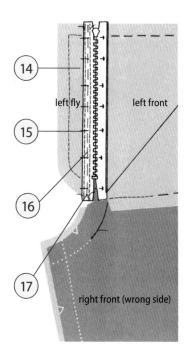

14. Press the center seam toward the fly, then place the garment on its left front and extend the fly.

15. Place the closed zipper face down on the left fly, with the bottom stop ¼ inch above the bottom of the seam opening, and the right edge of the tape on the pressed seam fold. Pin the left tape to the fly. If the tape extends above the top edge of the pants, cut it off according to the directions given on the zipper package.

16. Baste the zipper tape to the left fly ¼ inch from the teeth. Remove the pins.

17. Using a zipper foot, attach the zipper to the left fly with two rows of machine stitching, one row along the left edge of the basted tape and a second row close to the teeth.

CHAPTER 4: DETAILS OF GARMENT CONSTRUCTION

Finishing the Left Fly Front

18. With the pants wrong side down, fold under the left fly, causing the zipper to flip up. Pin the fly to the left front fabric at 1-inch intervals so that it lies flat.

19. Hand baste the left fly to the left front in a line 1½ inches from the folded edge. When you come to within 1½ inches of the bottom of the fly opening, curve the basting in to meet the center seam at the bottom of the opening. Do not catch the unstitched bottom end of the zipper tape in the stitches. Remove the pins.

20. Machine stitch the left fly to the left front, starting at the bottom curve just outside the basting. To reinforce the fly front, stitch forward two stitches, then back two stitches, and then forward to the waist. Remove all basting.

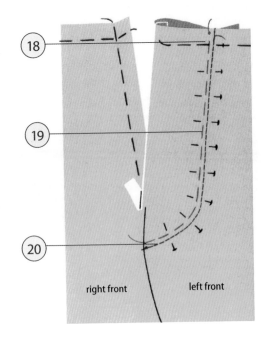

right front   left front

Basting the Zipper to the Right Front

21. Fold under the seam allowance of the right front along the basted fold line and press.

22. Place the folded edge of the right pants front over the zipper tape and pin at the top edges, making sure that the markings for the waist seam lines on both sections of the pants are aligned and that the zipper teeth extend just beyond the edge of the fold.

23. Opening the zipper as you proceed, pin the folded edge of the pants to the zipper tape close to the teeth.

24. Baste ¼ inch from the folded edge and remove the pins.

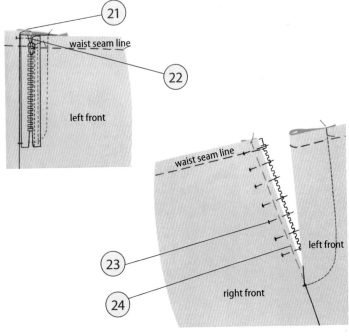

waist seam line

left front

waist seam line

left front

right front

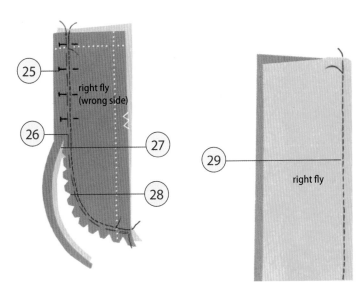

right fly
(wrong side)

right fly

25. With the wrong sides of the fabric facing outward, pin the two pieces of the right fly together along the long curved, unnotched edge.

26. Baste, remove the pins, and then machine stitch along the curved edge. Remove the bastings.

27. Trim the seam allowance of the stitched curved edge to ¼ inch.

28. Notch the curve of the trimmed seam allowance.

29. Turn the fly right side out and press the stitched seam flat. Topstitch with a line of machine stitching ⅛ inch from the sewn curved edge.

Attaching the Right Fly to the Right Pants Front

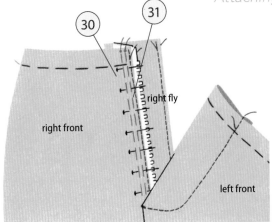

right fly

right front

left front

30. Lay the right pants front wrong side down over the right fly, setting the teeth ⅝ inch from the unstitched notched edge of the fly; pin to hold in place.

31. Baste from the bottom of the fly opening to the top, close to the folded edge. Remove the pins. Using a zipper foot, machine stitch, reinforcing the fly by stitching forward two stitches, then back two stitches and then forward the length of the zipper. Remove all bastings and press.

WAISTBANDS

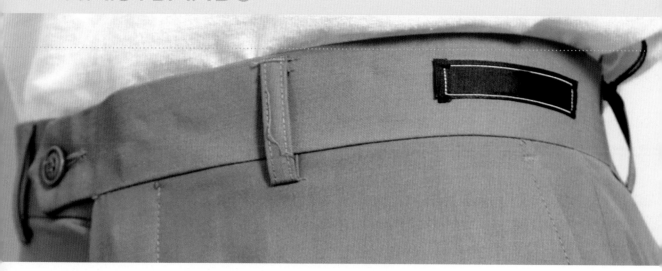

There are two marks of a well-made waistband: it lies flat without wrinkling or buckling, and it has a soft, rolled edge at the top. The secret to this look is in the way you handle the interfacing. Properly attached, by means of the method shown at right, the waistband should not crumple even when you move actively. And cutting and stitching above, rather than along, the center fold line gives the top edge a soft, professional finish.

Waistbands are fastened by hooks and eyes or buttons (*pages 162–171*) that are attached to an extension of the band called the lap. Many patterns call for an extension that overlaps at least ¾ inch across the opening of the pants or skirt. Some patterns, however, have an extension that underlaps the opening; the visible edge of the opening runs, then, in a straight line all the way up to the top of the waistband. The basic method of construction remains the same for both.

Preparing the Interfacing

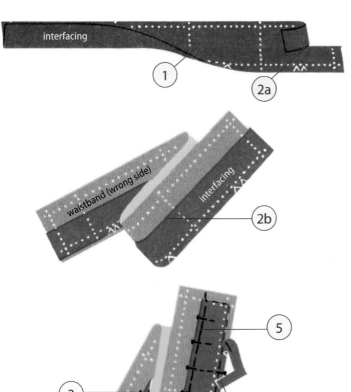

1. If the waistband and interfacing *(dark gray)* are cut from the same pattern piece, fold the interfacing in half lengthwise and mark a center fold line with chalk.

2a. Cutting ¼ inch above the center fold line, trim away the long part of the interfacing that has no pattern notches.

2b. If the interfacing has not been cut from the same pattern piece, make sure that it is the same length and ¼ inch more than half the width of the waistband.

Attaching the Interfacing

3. Place the interfacing on the wrong side of the waistband, lining it up with the notched edge. Pin together, matching the notches and pattern markings *(white)*.

4. Baste *(red)* the interfacing to the waistband along the notched side and both ends. Remove the pins.

5. Hand stitch *(black)* the interfacing to the waistband ⅛ inch above the center fold line, using thread the same color as the fabric. Make ½-inch stitches on the interfacing side but do not stitch through the waistband material; pick up only a thread of the waistband fabric.

6. Trim the interfacing close to the bastings along the three outer edges. Do not trim along the center fold line.

WAISTBANDS

Sewing the Waistband

7. Fold the waistband in half lengthwise, wrong side out.

8. Pin along the seam markings around the corner of the waistband, from the lap line to the folded edge. Then baste and remove the pins.

9. Machine stitch *(blue)* along the seam markings, from the lap line around the corner to the folded edge.

10. Pin the other end of the waistband together. Then baste along the end seam markings and remove the pins.

11. Machine stitch along the end seam markings, beginning at the corner where the end and long seam markings intersect—not at the edge of the fabric.

12. Clip into the seam allowance diagonally at the lap line, cutting close to but not into the stitching.

13. At the lapped end. trim the seam allowance to ¼ inch and trim both corners diagonally.

14. Trim the seam allowance at the other end of the waistband to ¼ inch and trim diagonally at the folded edge.

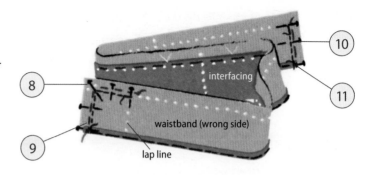

interfacing

waistband (wrong side)

lap line

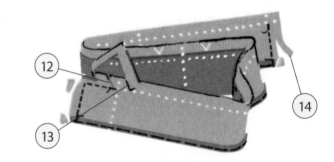

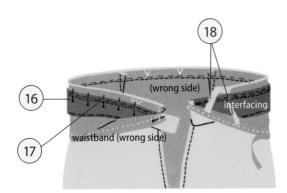

15. Turn the waistband and the garment right sides out.

16. Pin the long notched edge of the waistband to the garment along the waist seam-line markings, matching notches and seams. Be sure the sides of the waistband and garment fabric that will be visible in the finished garment are facing each other.

17. Baste along the waist seam-line markings. Remove the pins, and then machine stitch.

18. Trim the garment seam allowance to ⅛ inch. Trim the waistband seam allowance to ¼ inch. Trim the seam allowance of the long unstitched waistband edge to ¼ inch.

The Final Touches

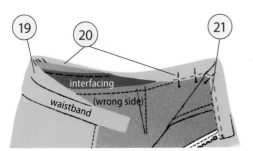

19. Turn over the long unstitched edge of the waistband to the inside of the garment.

20. Fold under the unstitched edge along the seam markings and pin it to the garment, then baste and remove the pins.

21. Hand stitch the folded edge of the waistband to the garment with a slip stitch *(page 25)*. Do not stitch into the garment fabric but pick up only a few threads of the seam allowance. Remove all bastings and press.

SLEEVES AND CUFFS

Two classic sleeves are the tailored sleeve for shirts and the soft sleeve for blouses. They are distinguished partly by their cuffs—the tailored cuff is made of two separate pieces crisply stitched together along the outside edges; the blouse cuff is cut in one piece and folded under at the edge. But with either type of sleeve, nothing is more important than a smooth set-in look at the armhole.

The smooth armhole attachment is easiest to achieve with the tailored sleeve. It goes into its body section quite simply because both are cut full to allow for freedom of movement. Because there is little difference between the size of the sleeve and the armhole, the sleeve can be attached in one long seam before assembling sleeve or body section.

The body section of a blouse fits more closely and its armhole is therefore relatively smaller than its sleeve, which needs enough fullness to allow the arm to move freely. This fullness must be reduced, or eased, as the sleeve is sewn into the armhole of an assembled garment.

The key to a smoothly set-in sleeve is the ease basting; make double lines of machine basting rather than a single line to guide you in controlling the fullness at the sleeve cap.

Preparing the Cuff Opening

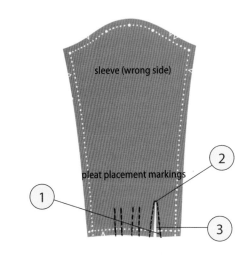

1. To reinforce the area around the cuff opening, called the placket, machine stitch (blue)—without backstitching—from the bottom right edge of the pattern marking for the placket to the placket point, using 15 stitches per inch.

2. Raise the presser foot on your machine, turn the sleeve slightly, lower the presser foot and take one stitch across the placket point. Then raise the presser foot again, turn further, lower the presser foot and continue stitching down the other side of the placket.

3. Cut a straight line up the middle of the V formed by the stitching, cutting to the placket point.

Attaching the Strip of Fabric to the Placket

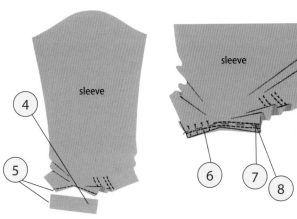

4. From fabric left over after you cut out the pattern, cut a strip along the lengthwise grain 1½ inches wide and twice the length of the closed placket.

5. Lay the strip wrong side down, spread open the placket, and place it wrong side down over the strip, aligning the ends of the placket with the outer corners of the strip.

6. Pin the strip to the placket, with the point of the placket ¼ inch in from the outer edge of the strip.

7. Baste (red) the strip to the placket, and remove the pins.

8. Machine stitch—resetting the machine to the normal 12 stitches per inch—in a straight line along the placket just inside the reinforcement stitches made in Step 1, pausing at the placket point to move the bunched-up fabric out of the way. Remove the basting.

9. Pull the unstitched edge of the strip from under the placket so that the strip projects wrong side up.

10. Press the seam allowance over the projecting strip.

11. Fold in the outer edge of the strip ¼ inch and press.

SLEEVES AND CUFFS: FOR A TAILORED SHIRT

Enclosing the Placket

12. Pin the folded outer edge of the strip to the placket so that it just covers the lines of machine stitching.

13. Baste and remove the pins.

14. Machine stitch along the folded edge, spreading the placket farther open as you go; pause at the point of the placket to redistribute the bunched-up fabric. Remove the basting and press.

15. Turn the sleeve over so that it is wrong side up.

16. Fold one side under along the placket line. Without backstitching, machine stitch on a diagonal from the point of the placket to a spot ¼ inch down on its outer edge.

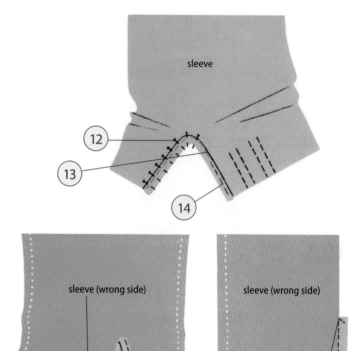

Pleating the Bottom of the Sleeve

17. To make pleats at the places indicated on the pattern, turn the sleeve right side up, to the side that will be visible in the finished garment, and open it out flat.

18. Fold the pleats along their markings (green) toward the placket, then pin them.

19. Turn under the front lap of the placket—that is, the side closest to the pleats—and hold it and the pleats in place by basting along the bottom stitching line. Remove the pins.

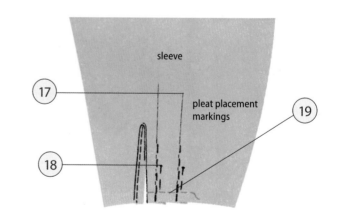

SLEEVES AND CUFFS: FOR A TAILORED SHIRT

Attaching the Sleeve to the Body Section

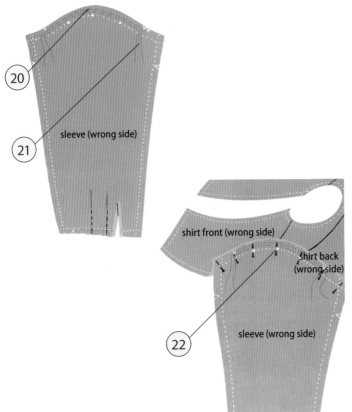

20. Turn the sleeve wrong side out. Machine baste—six stitches per inch—between the pattern markings *(white)* that indicate where extra fabric will be eased, making two parallel lines of basting ¼ inch apart along the top of the sleeve.

21. Pull the loose threads gently, first at one end, then at the other, to distribute the easing evenly.

22. Pin the sleeve to the armhole of the shirt body, all sections wrong sides out, matching dots, notches and seam intersections.

sleeve (wrong side)

shirt front (wrong side)

shirt back (wrong side)

sleeve (wrong side)

Stitching the Sleeve to the Body Section

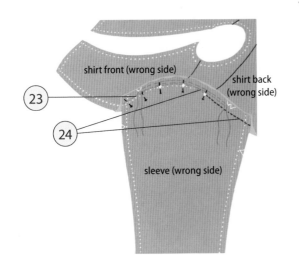

shirt front (wrong side)

shirt back (wrong side)

sleeve (wrong side)

23. Distribute the eased fabric evenly until the sleeve fits smoothly into the armhole. Add pins as necessary.

24. Baste the sleeve to the body section, remove the pins, then machine stitch. Remove the basting, but leave in the ease lines.

25. Press both seam allowances toward the body section. Turn the garment right side out and press again.

26. Turn the garment wrong side out and construct a flat felled seam *(page 94)* around the armhole.

SLEEVES AND CUFFS: FOR A TAILORED SHIRT

Making the Side Seam

27. With the wrong sides of the fabric facing out, bring the side and underarm seams together, and pin the front of the body section to the back at the intersection of the armhole seam.

28. Pin the underarm seam of the sleeve, then pin the side seam of the body section, matching the notches.

29. Baste along the underarm seam and the side seam in one continuous line. Remove the pins.

30. Machine stitch from the bottom of the sleeve to the shirttail in one continuous line. Remove the basting.

31. Press both seam allowances toward the back of the garment and construct a continuous flat felled seam (page 94) along the sleeve and body section.

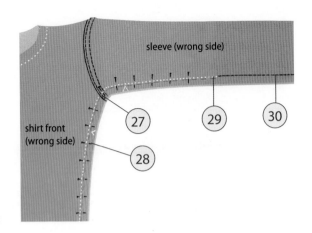

sleeve (wrong side)

shirt front (wrong side)

Attaching the Interfacing and Facing to the Cuff

32. Lay the cuff down wrong side up. Place the interfacing (dark gray) on top and pin together.

33. Baste just outside the stitching line. Remove the pins.

34. Trim away the interfacing all around the basting.

35. Fold in the top edge of the cuff along the stitching line and press.

36. Trim the folded edge to ¼ inch.

37. Place the cuff facing wrong side down and cover with the interfaced cuff wrong side up. Pin together.

38. Baste along the three outer sides, leaving the folded edge open. Remove the pins.

39. Machine stitch along the three basted sides.

40. Trim the seam allowance to ¼ inch around the three stitched sides; the facing will extend on the fourth side of the cuff. Remove the basting.

41. If the cuff is rounded, clip into the corners.

42. Turn the cuff right side out and press it and its extended facing flat.

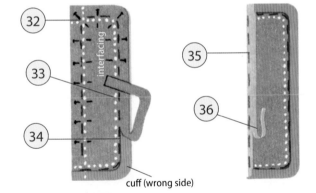

interfacing

cuff (wrong side)

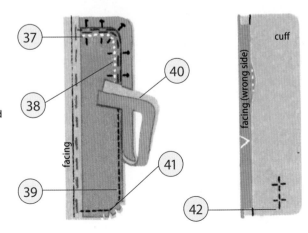

facing

cuff

facing (wrong side)

Attaching the Cuff to the Sleeve

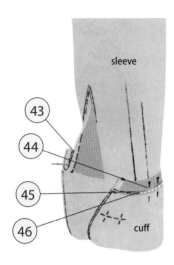

43. Turn the sleeve right side out and curl up the bottom edge.

44. Holding the cuff so that the wrong side of the facing is toward you, pin the extension of the cuff facing to the curled-up bottom of the sleeve. Match notches.

45. Hand baste the cuff facing to the sleeve, then remove the pins.

46. Machine stitch the facing to the sleeve, following the stitching line. Remove the basting.

Completing the Cuff

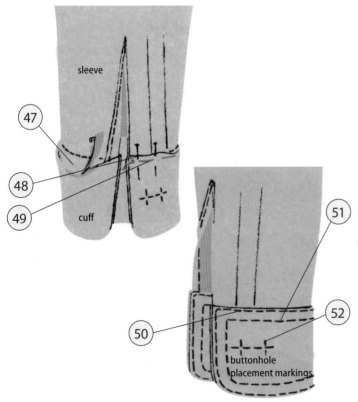

47. Slip the bottom seam allowances between the cuff facing and interfacing. Press, then trim to ¼ inch.

48. Pin the folded edge of the cuff just over the stitching line of the sleeve.

49. Hand baste, then remove the pins.

50. Machine stitch along the folded edge *(Edge Stitching, page 15)*, sewing at the top of the cuff from one edge of the placket to the other. Then pivot the cuff in the machine and stitch all along the outer edge of the cuff. When you reach the top edge of the cuff again, secure the last stitches by backstitching. Remove the basting.

51. Machine stitch a second line all around the cuff ¼ inch in from the stitching line made in Step 50 *(Topstitching, page 15)*.

52. Following the basted pattern markings for buttonhole positions, make buttonholes and attach buttons *(pages 162–169)*.

53. Repeat the preceding steps on the other sleeve.

Preparing the Cuff Opening

1. Reinforce *(blue)* the area around the cuff opening, called the placket, as in the instructions for a tailored shirt *(page 121, Steps 1 and 2)*, making two or three stitches at the top of the placket to form a U shape rather than the V shape of the tailored shirt.

2. Cut a straight line up the middle of the U formed by the stitching, cutting to the top of the placket.

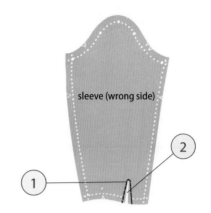

sleeve (wrong side)

Attaching the Strip of Fabric to the Placket

3. From fabric left over after cutting out the pattern, cut a strip along the lengthwise grain 1½ inches wide and twice the length of the closed placket.

4. Lay the strip wrong side down, spread open the placket and place it wrong side up over the strip, aligning the ends of the placket with the outer corners of the strip.

5. Pin, then baste *(red)* the strip to the placket, with the curve of the placket ¼ inch in from the strip's outer edge. Remove the pins.

6. Machine stitch—resetting the machine to the normal 12 stitches per inch—in a straight line along the placket inside the reinforcement stitches made in Step 1, pausing at the placket curve to move the bunched-up fabric out of the way. Remove the basting.

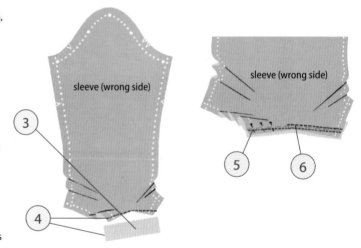

sleeve (wrong side)

sleeve (wrong side)

7. Pull the unstitched edge of the strip from under the placket so that the strip projects wrong side up.

8. Press the seam allowance over the projecting strip.

9. Fold in the outer edge of the strip ¼ inch and press.

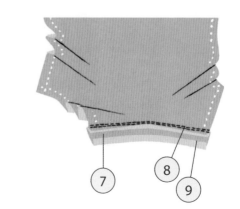

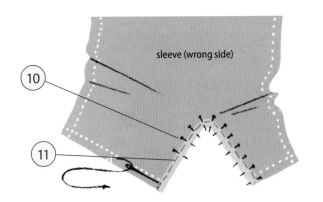

sleeve (wrong side)

10. Pin the folded edge of the strip to the placket so that it just covers the lines of machine stitching.

11. Baste close to the fold, then remove the pins and press.

12. Hand stitch *(black)* with a hemming stitch *(page 22)* along the edge. Do not stitch into the fabric beneath the folded edge but pick up only the thread from the machine stitching made in Step 6. Remove the basting.

13. Spread the placket open and press on the wrong side.

14. With the sleeve still wrong side up, fold one side under along the placket line.

15. Without backstitching, machine stitch on a diagonal from the top curve of the placket to a spot ¼ inch down on its outer edge.

16. Turn back the front lap of the placket—on the wider part of the sleeve—and baste a few stitches along the seam allowance to secure the lap to the sleeve.

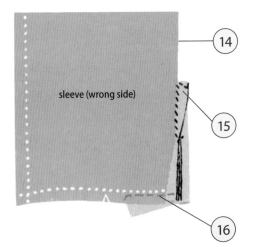

sleeve (wrong side)

SLEEVES AND CUFFS: FOR A WOMAN'S BLOUSE

Making the Sleeve Seam

17. Open the sleeve out flat, wrong side up, and machine baste—six stitches per inch—between the pattern markings *(white)* used to indicate the area where extra fabric will be eased, making two parallel lines ¼ inch apart along the top of the sleeve.

18. Fold the sleeve in half, wrong sides out, and pin along the underarm seam, matching and pinning first at the seam intersection, next at the notches, then at any other pattern markings. Add more pins at 1- to 2-inch intervals.

19. Baste from the armhole to the end of the sleeve, then remove the pins.

20. Machine stitch—resetting the machine to the normal 12 stitches per inch—from the armhole to the end of the sleeve, then remove the basting.

21. Press the seam open on a sleeve board.

22. Make two parallel ease lines ¼ inch apart, as in Step 17, in the seam allowance at the bottom of the sleeve, starting and ending ½ inch from the placket.

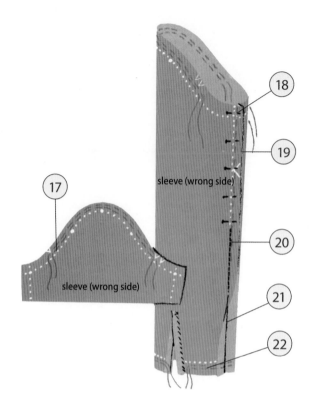

Attaching the Interfacing to the Cuff

23. Lay the cuff down, wrong side up. Place the interfacing *(dark gray)* on top and pin the two together on the three outer sides, matching notches or other pattern markings. Leave the inside edge open.

24. Baste the three outer sides just outside the stitching line. Remove the pins, and trim the interfacing.

25. Attach the open edge of the interfacing to the cuff using a hemming stitch *(page 22)*.

26. On the half of the cuff that has no interfacing, fold in the outer edge along the stitching line. Press, and trim the folded edge to ¼ inch.

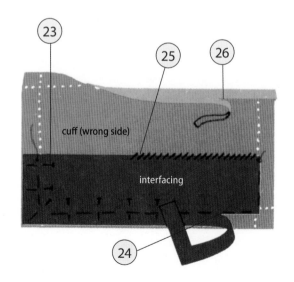

Attaching the Cuff to the Sleeve

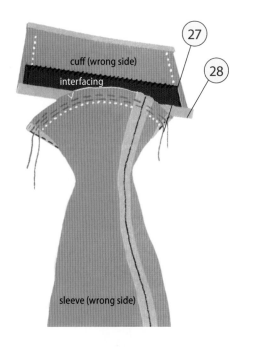

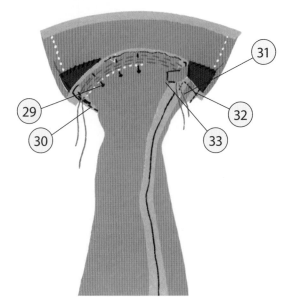

27. With the sleeve wrong side out, gently pull the loose ease threads sewn in Step 22 to begin adjusting the ease.

28. Turn up the bottom of the interfaced half of the cuff.

29. Pin the sleeve to the cuff along its turned-up edge, matching notches.

30. Align the stitching lines of the cuff edges with the outer edges of the placket; if your pattern calls for the cuff to extend beyond the placket, disregard the cuff stitching lines on the extension and match notches and other pattern markings.

31. To ease the sleeve into the cuff, pull the loose ease threads, first at one end, then at the other, gradually distributing the easing until the sleeve fits the cuff. Secure with additional pins at ½-inch intervals.

32. Hand baste just below the ease lines. Remove the pins and machine stitch.

33. Trim the two layers of the seam allowance—sleeve and cuff—¼ inch from the stitching line. Remove the basting, then press the trimmed seam allowance toward the cuff.

SLEEVES AND CUFFS: FOR A WOMAN'S BLOUSE

Stitching the Ends of the Cuff

34. Turn the sleeve right side out. Fold the cuff in half along its fold line so that it is wrong side out.

35. Pin the open ends of the cuff together and baste. Remove the pins.

36. Machine stitch the ends together, sewing a few stitches off the edge of the fabric. Tie off the threads.

37. Trim the seam allowances to ¼ inch and remove the basting.

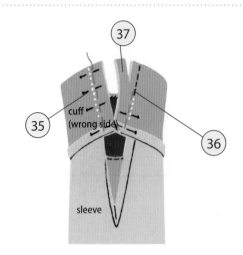

Completing the Cuff

38. Turn the sleeve wrong side out. Turn the cuff right side out.

39. Pin the edge of the cuff over the stitching line of the sleeve and baste. Remove the pins.

40. Stitch the cuff to the sleeve with a hemming stitch *(page 22)* along the edge. Do not stitch into the fabric beneath the folded edge but pick up only the thread from the machine stitching made in Step 32. Remove the basting.

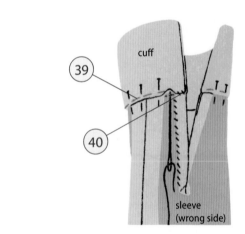

Inserting the Sleeve into the Armhole

41. Pull the ease lines made in Step 17 at the top of the sleeve, distributing the easing evenly.

42. Turn the sleeve right side out and slip it into the armhole of the body section of the blouse, which should be wrong side out.

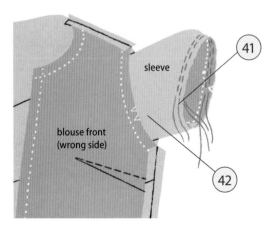

Connecting the Sleeve to the Armhole

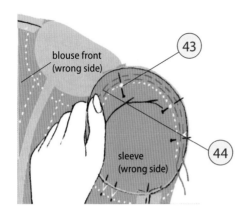

43. Roll the top of the sleeve over the armhole of the body section, and pin, matching the center marking at the top of the sleeve to the shoulder seam, and aligning the seams under the arm, the notches and other pattern markings.

44. With the two layers of fabric rolled over your forefingers, redistribute the extra fabric of the sleeve.

Stitching the Sleeve to the Armhole

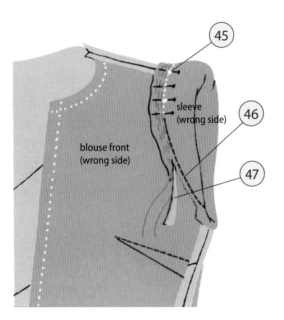

45. With the wrong side of the sleeve rolled over the shoulder, pin and baste all around the armhole, starting at the underarm seam. Remove the pins.

46. Machine stitch and remove the basting. Press.

47. Trim the seam allowance to ½ inch except under the arm, where it should be tapered to ¼ inch. Press.

48. Following the pattern markings *(green)* on the cuff for buttonhole positions, make buttonholes and attach buttons to the cuff *(pages 162–169)*.

49. Repeat the preceding steps on the other sleeve.

Chapter 4: DETAILS OF GARMENT CONSTRUCTION

COLLARS

There are two classic collars. One is the familiar man's shirt collar, known as a two-piece stand-up collar, or a collar with a band. In fact it is constructed with six pieces: the collar and the undercollar, with interfacing between, and the outer and inner neckbands, with interfacing. The man's collar is frequently favored by women for use on their tailored shirts and shirtwaist dresses.

The second classic collar is designed for more casual wear, open. It is sometimes called the Italian collar, or the convertible collar. It is constructed with only three pieces, the collar and the undercollar and an interfacing. It attaches to the garment without an intervening neckband.

Interfacing the Collar

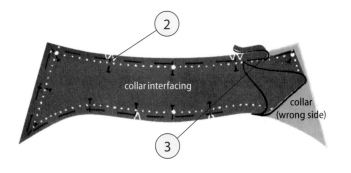

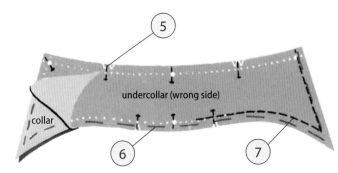

1. Assemble the pieces you will need to interface the collar: the piece that will be visible, called simply the collar; the under part of the collar known as the undercollar; and the interfacing that will be stitched between the two to provide stiffening.

2. Pin and baste *(red)* the collar interfacing to the wrong side of the collar, matching the pattern markings *(white)*. Remove the pins.

3. Trim the interfacing just above the basting along the neckline only.

4. Turn the collar over so that the interfacing lies on the table and the right side of the collar, the side that will be visible in the finished garment, faces up.

5. Place the undercollar, wrong side up, on top of the collar. Pin together, matching the pattern markings.

6. Baste the undercollar to the collar along the two ends and the curved bottom edge. Leave the upper neck edge open. Remove the pins.

7. Machine stitch *(blue)* alongside the basting. Remove the basting.

COLLARS: THE SHIRT COLLAR

Completing the Collar

8. Turn the assembled collar over, interfacing up.

9. Trim the interfacing as close as possible to the stitching made in Step 7.

10. Trim the seam allowance of the collar to ¼ inch along the sides and bottom edge.

11. Trim the seam allowance of the undercollar to ⅛ inch along the sides and bottom edge.

12. Trim the collar points diagonally, following the instructions on page 95, Step 4.

13. Clip the trimmed seam allowances of the bottom edge of the collar assembly at ½-inch intervals.

14. Turn the assembled collar right side out so that the interfacing lies between collar and undercollar, gently pushing out the points with closed scissors; pull the points out farther from the outside with a pin.

15. Open the collar assembly from the unstitched neck edge as far as possible and press the seams open from the inside.

16. Gently roll the outside of the collar seams between your fingers to bring the stitching out to the edge. Roll again lightly so that the seam stitching is turned 1/16 inch onto the undercollar side and baste to hold in place. Press.

17. Make a line of edge stitching and/or topstitching around the seamed edges if desired (page 15).

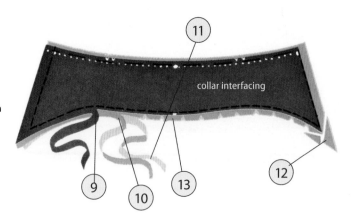

collar interfacing

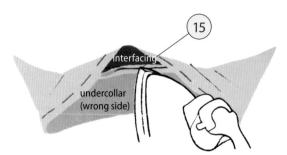

interfacing

undercollar (wrong side)

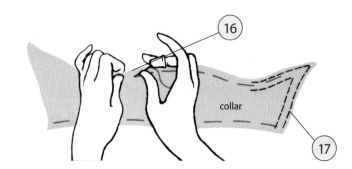

collar

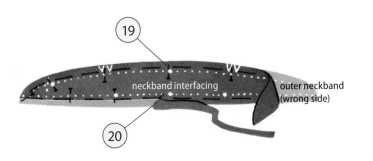

neckband interfacing

outer neckband
(wrong side)

18. Lay out the pieces you will need to attach the collar to the neckband—the assembled interfaced collar (just completed), the outer neckband, the inner neckband and the interfacing that will be stitched between them to stiffen the neckband.

19. Pin and baste the neckband interfacing to the wrong side of the outer neckband, matching the pattern markings. Remove the pins.

20. Trim the interfacing close to the basting along the straighter edge *(bottom edge in drawing).*

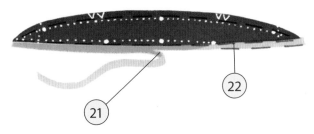

21. Trim the outer neckband along the straighter edge, ¼ inch from the trimmed interfacing.

22. Turn up the straighter edge of the outer neckband along the seam line, and baste it against the interfacing. Press.

Attaching the Outer Neckband to the Collar

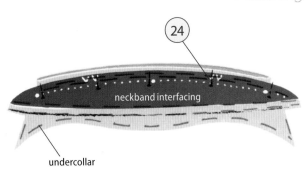

neckband interfacing

undercollar

23. Place the collar assembly on your table so that the undercollar faces up and the neck edge is at top. Lay the outer neckband on top of it with the interfacing up so that the edge with curved ends is at top.

24. Pin the neck edge of the collar assembly to the edge of the inner neckband having curved ends; match the pattern markings. Begin pinning in the center of the collar assembly and work toward each side. Baste, and remove the pins.

COLLARS: THE SHIRT COLLAR

Attaching the Inner Neckband to the Collar

25. Turn the collar assembly and outer neckband over so that the undercollar part of the assembled collar faces down and the outer neckband, wrong side down, is hidden underneath it.

26. Then place the inner neckband, wrong side up, on the collar. Pin and baste the curved-end edge of the inner neckband *(at top in the drawing)* to the unstitched neck edge of the collar, matching the pattern markings. Remove the pins.

27. Machine stitch alongside the basting, then remove all bastings.

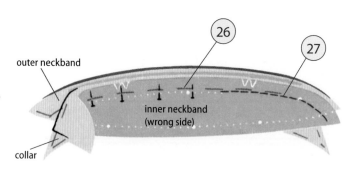

outer neckband

inner neckband
(wrong side)

collar

Completing the Collar and Neckband

28. Turn the collar over so that the undercollar and neckband interfacing face up.

29. Trim the seam allowance of the interfacing close to the stitching line.

30. Trim the collar assembly seam allowances to ⅛ inch.

31. Trim the inner and outer neckband seam allowances to ¼ inch.

32. Clip all the trimmed seam allowances at ½ inch intervals along the middle and notch at ½ inch intervals along the ends, where the curve is more pronounced.

33. Turn the neckband right side out and press.

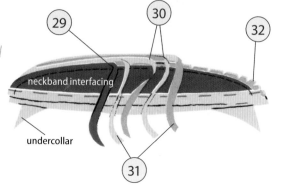

neckband interfacing

undercollar

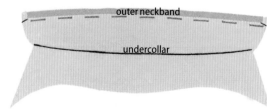

inner neckband
(wrong side)

outer neckband

undercollar

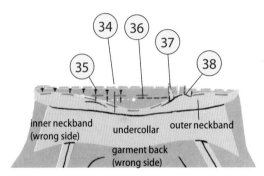

inner neckband
(wrong side)   undercollar   outer neckband

garment back
(wrong side)

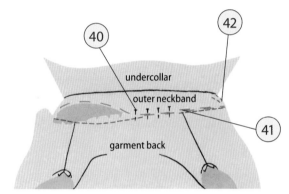

undercollar

outer neckband

garment back

34. Open the garment out flat, wrong side up with the neck edge at top. Clip the seam allowance of the neck edge of the garment at ½-inch intervals close to the stay stitching.

35. Spread the neckband open. Pin the inner neckband to the wrong side of the garment's neck edge. Begin pinning on the center of the neckband and work toward each side, matching the pattern markings. Baste and remove the pins.

36. Machine stitch and remove the basting.

37. Trim the inner neckband seam allowance to ⅛ inch.

38. Trim the garment neck edge seam allowance to ¼ inch.

39. Turn the garment right side out. Press the garment neck edge and inner neckband seam allowances inside the neckband up toward the collar.

40. Pin and baste the outer neckband to the garment, covering the stitches made in Step 36. Remove the pins.

41. Machine stitch as close to the bottom edges of the neckband as possible from one end to the other. Remove the basting.

42. Run a line of decorative edge stitching and/or topstitching on the outer neckband if desired.

Making the Collar

1. Make the convertible collar following the instructions for the tailored collar Steps 1–17 *(pages 133–134)*, but omitting Step 13.

2. Clip into the neck edge seam allowance of the collar assembly at each of the two shoulder markings *(white)*.

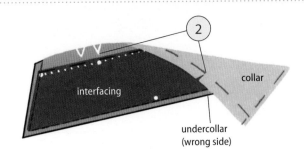

collar

interfacing

undercollar
(wrong side)

Attaching the Collar to the Garment

3. Clip the seam allowance around the neck edge of the garment at ½ inch intervals, cutting close to the stay stitching as shown in blue.

4. Pin the collar assembly to the outside of the garment at the neck edge, matching center back, shoulder and center front markings. Begin pinning in the center of the undercollar and work toward each side. Do not pin the collar seam allowance between the shoulder markings or the front facings.

5. Baste *(red)* along the neck edge from one front edge of the collar to the clip marking at the shoulder. At the clipped shoulder marking, fold down the seam allowance of the collar. Then continue to baste across to the other edge; do not catch the loose seam allowance of the collar when basting between the two shoulder seams. Remove the pins.

6. Fold both front facings of the garment back along the fold lines and pin and baste the facings to the collar, matching pattern markings. Remove the pins.

7. Machine stitch the entire length of the neck edge. Be sure not to catch the loose seam allowance of the collar when stitching between the shoulder seams. Remove the basting.

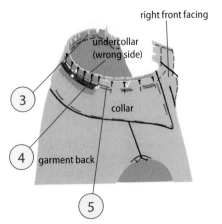

right front facing

undercollar
(wrong side)

collar

garment back

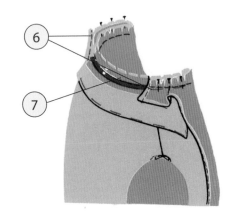

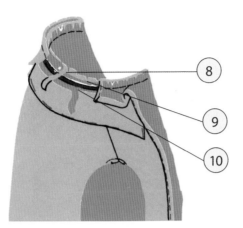

8. Spread apart the seam allowances of the facing and garment neck edge, then trim the collar assembly seam allowance to ⅛ inch. Be careful not to cut the folded down section of collar seam allowance.

9. Trim the facings and garment neck edge to ¼ inch.

10. Trim the seam allowance of the unstitched portion of the collar between the shoulders to ¼ inch.

Finishing the Collar

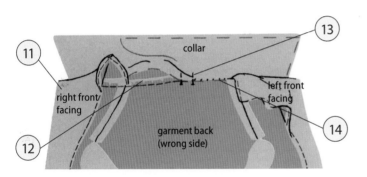

collar

right front facing

garment back (wrong side)

left front facing

11. Turn the facings right side out, pushing the points into shape with the points of closed scissors. Press.

12. Press the stitched seam allowance between the shoulders up toward the undercollar.

13. Turn under the trimmed seam allowance of the collar along its stitching line. Pin the collar over the trimmed neck edge seam allowance, just covering the stitches.

14. Baste, then remove the pins and slip stitch (black) as illustrated on page 25. Remove all bastings and press.

HEMS AND FACING

Facings and hems finish and conceal raw edges by turning them inside the garment. The most important thing to remember about facings is that if the garment has been altered in the area where a facing will be stitched, the facing, and interfacing if there is any, should be altered in precisely the same way to ensure a proper fit.

Hemming is the last step in constructing trouser legs and sleeves that do not have cuffs, as well as dresses. Legs and sleeves are fairly easy: try the garment on before a mirror and pin up one or two places by eye. Take the garment off, measure the distance between the pin and the raw edge, turn the edge under evenly all around, and sew it as shown in the drawings opposite.

Hemming a dress is somewhat more involved. First, hang it up overnight. Next day, put on the shoes you plan to wear with the dress, stand on the floor (not a deep carpet) in a natural posture and measure from the floor up. Pin or make a chalk mark every 3 inches around the bottom edge. Then construct the hem as shown on the following pages. To guide you in determining the proper depth of the hem, the general rule is: the heavier the fabric or the more flared the skirt, the narrower the hem of the garment should be.

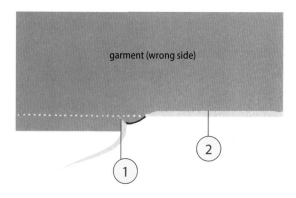

garment (wrong side)

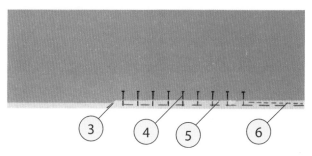

1. With the garment wrong side out, trim the raw hem edge evenly along the cutting line *(white)*.

2. Turn the hem edge up ¼ inch and press flat.

3. Turn the hem up again ½ inch.

4. Pin the hem to the garment at 1-inch intervals.

5. Baste *(red)* through all layers of the fabric ⅛ inch from the folded edge of the hem made in Step 2. Remove the pins.

6. Machine stitch *(blue)* the hem to the garment close to the basting made in Step 5. If a hand finish is desired, use a slip stitch for woven fabrics or a catch stitch for knits. Remove the basting.

Chapter 4: DETAILS OF GARMENT CONSTRUCTION

Turning up the Hem

1. After marking with pins or chalk the hem length most suitable to your figure, turn the garment wrong side out. Then turn the bottom edge up along the pinned or chalk-marked hemline.

2. Pin the hem to the garment, matching seams, at 1-inch intervals close to the hem fold.

3. Pin every 6 inches near the raw hem edge. Try on the garment; adjust and re-pin the hemline if necessary.

4. Baste (red) the hem to the garment ½ inch from the bottom. Then remove all pins.

5. Trim the raw hem edge so the hem is even and no deeper than 2½ inches. Press.

6. If the garment is slightly flared, ease the excess fullness of the raw edge of the hem following the directions on page 92–93.

Finishing the Hem Edge

7. For woven fabrics, turn the garment right side out. Unfold the hem and pin seam tape to the hem edge so that the tape extends ¼ inch beyond the raw edge of the hem. Pin at 1-inch intervals beginning at a seam.

8. Finish ½ inch beyond the starting point, and turn the tape end under ¼ inch.

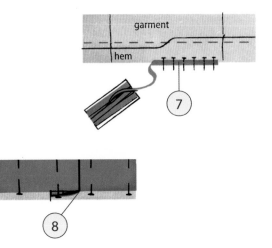

garment (wrong side)

hem

garment

hem

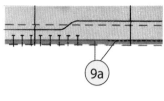

9a. Baste and remove the pins. Machine stitch *(blue)* the tape to the hem close to the bottom edge of the tape. Remove the basting.

9b. For nonravelly knits, turn the garment right side out. Unfold the hem and machine stitch a line ¼ inch from the trimmed raw hem edge.

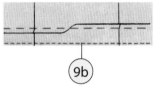 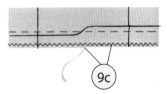

9c. For ravelly knits and woven fabrics, turn the garment right side out. Unfold the hem and make a line of zigzag stitching ¼ inch from the trimmed hem edge; then trim close to the stitching.

Completing the Hem

10. Re-pin the hem to the garment fabric, placing pins at 2-inch intervals parallel to and ½ inch below the finished edge.

11. Baste the hem to the garment and remove the pins.

12. Hand stitch *(black)* the hem to the garment. Use a hemming stitch for woven fabrics or a catch stitch for knits *(pages 22 and 24)*. Remove bastings and press.

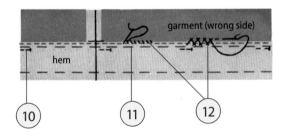

garment (wrong side)

hem

1. To hem a garment with a faced and interfaced opening that extends to the bottom of the hem, turn the garment wrong side out, unfold the facing and press it flat.

2. Turn up the hem, finish the raw hem edge and sew the hem to the garment, following Steps 1–12 on pages 142–143. Be sure to stitch the hem all the way to the outer edge of the facing; however, if seam tape is used to finish the hem edge, cut that off at the front fold-line bastings to reduce bulk.

3. Turn the facing to the inside of the garment, folding along the front fold-line bastings *(green)*. Press lightly.

4. Pin the facing to the hem around the corner as shown, and hand stitch *(black)* in place with a slip stitch *(page 25)*. Remove the pins.

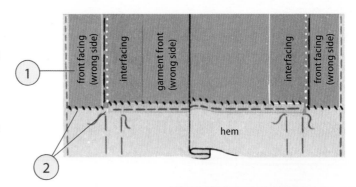

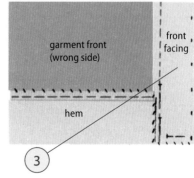

Preparing the Facing

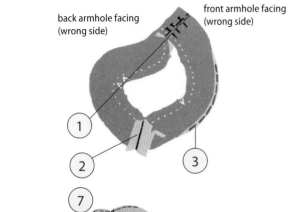

back armhole facing
(wrong side)

front armhole facing
(wrong side)

1. Cut and mark the front and back armhole facing pieces. With the wrong sides facing out, pin together the front and back facing pieces along the underarm and the shoulder seam markings *(white)*. Baste *(red)*, remove the pins and machine stitch *(blue)* the shoulder and underarm seams. Remove the basting.

2. Press open both seams and trim to ½ inch.

3. Finish the unnotched edge of the facing as you would any seam *(page 90)*, or turn the edge over ¼ inch and press flat. Then machine stitch ⅛ inch from the fold.

Attaching the Facing to the Garment

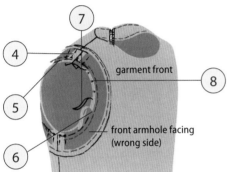

garment front

front armhole facing
(wrong side)

4. Turn the garment right side out and pin the facing—wrong side out—to it along the armhole seam markings. Pin at notches and seam intersections, then at ½-inch intervals. Baste and remove the pins.

5. Machine stitch along seam markings, beginning and ending at the intersection between the underarm and armhole seams. Remove the basting.

6. Trim the facing armhole seam allowance to ⅛ inch.

7. Trim the garment armhole seam allowance to ¼ inch.

8. Clip into both armhole seam allowances at ½-inch intervals, cutting close to but not into the stitching.

9. Turn the garment wrong side out.

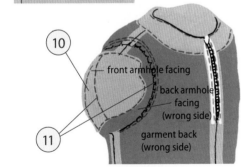

front armhole facing

back armhole facing
(wrong side)

garment back
(wrong side)

10. Turn the facing up so that it extends away from the garment and press the armhole seam allowances toward the facing.

11. Understitch the facing and seam allowances as shown for the round neck facing, Step 21 *(page 149)*. Begin and end at the underarm seam.

Hand Finishing the Facing

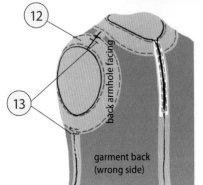

back armhole facing

garment back
(wrong side)

12. Turn the facing down over the wrong side of the garment and press flat.

13. Pin the facing to the garment at the shoulder and underarm seams as shown and attach the facing to those seam allowances with a slip stitch *(black)*. Remove the pins and press.

Preparing the Garment

1. If you have not already done so, machine stitch *(blue)* along the seam-line markings *(white)* at the neck of each garment section to prevent the neckline from pulling out of shape as you work *(page 14)*.

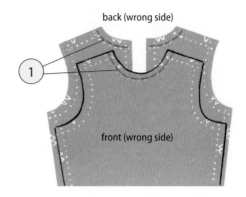

back (wrong side)

front (wrong side)

Preparing the Interfacing

2. If your interfacings *(dark gray)* were cut from special interfacing pattern pieces, not from the same pattern pieces used for the facings, skip Step 2 and go on to Step 3. If facings and interfacings were cut from the same pattern pieces, trim away ⅜ inch from the unnotched edges of the interfacing.

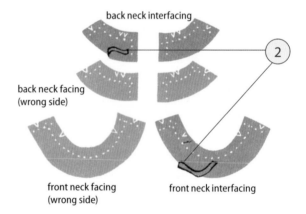

back neck interfacing

back neck facing
(wrong side)

front neck facing
(wrong side)

front neck interfacing

Basting the Interfacing to the Garment

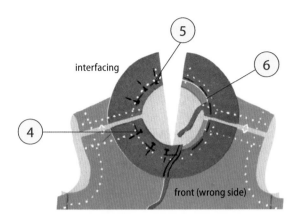

interfacing

front (wrong side)

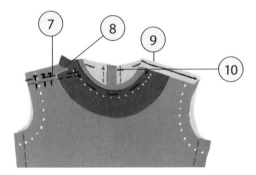

3. Adjust your garment for fit, and make corresponding adjustments to your interfacing.

4. Pin the interfacing pieces to the wrong sides of the garment sections along the neck seam-line markings, matching notches and shoulder seam lines.

5. Baste *(red)* the interfacings to the garment outside the neck seam line; begin and end at the neck and shoulder seam intersections. Do not sew to the ends of the interfacings. Remove the pins.

6. Trim the interfacing around the neckline close to the bastings.

7. Pin and baste the shoulder seams along the seam-line markings. Remove the pins, machine stitch and remove the bastings.

8. Trim the interfacing ends along the shoulder seams ⅛ inch from the stitching.

9. Press open the shoulder seams; trim to ½ inch.

10. Insert the zipper *(Centered Zipper, page 108)*.

Preparing the Facing

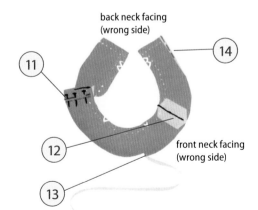

back neck facing
(wrong side)

front neck facing
(wrong side)

11. With the wrong sides of the fabric facing out, pin and baste together the back and front neck facing pieces along the shoulder seam markings. Remove the pins, machine stitch the shoulder seams and remove the basting.

12. Press open the seams and trim to ½ inch.

13. Trim the unnotched curved edge of the facing to make an even curve.

14. Finish the unnotched edge as you would any seam *(page 90)*, or turn the edge under ¼ inch, press flat and machine stitch ⅛ inch from the fold.

Attaching the Facing to the Garment

15. Turn the garment right side out and pin the facing wrong side out to it along the neck seam-line markings. Make notches and shoulder seams on the facing align with those on the garment. Pin first at notches and seam intersections, then at ½ inch intervals in between.

16. Baste the facing to the garment along the neck seam line. Remove the pins, machine stitch the neck seam. Remove all neckline bastings.

17. Trim the facing seam allowance around the neckline to ⅛ inch.

18. Trim the garment seam allowance around the neckline to ¼ inch.

19. Clip into all neckline seam allowances every ½ inch around the curve. Cut close to but not into the line of stitching.

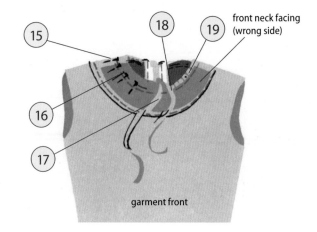

front neck facing
(wrong side)

garment front

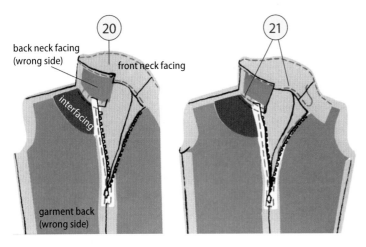

back neck facing
(wrong side)

front neck facing

interfacing

garment back
(wrong side)

20. Turn the garment wrong side out. Lift the facing so it extends away from the garment and press the neckline seam allowances toward the facing.

21. Slide the facing, wrong side down, under the sewing machine presser foot and make a line of stitching—called understitching—close to the neckline seam. Be sure the understitching catches the seam allowances beneath the facing fabric.

Finishing the Facing

22. Turn the facing down over the wrong side of the garment and press flat.

23. Pin the facing to the garment at the shoulder seams and attach it there with a slip stitch *(page 25)* shown in black. Remove the pins.

24. Fold under the center back ends of the facing so that they clear the zipper teeth. Pin and sew the fold with a slip stitch. Remove the pins and press.

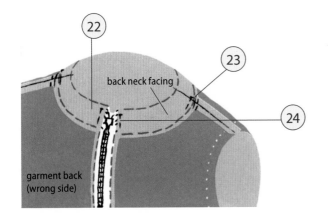

back neck facing

garment back
(wrong side)

Preparing the Garment and Interfacing

1. If you have not already done so, reinforce *(blue)* the neckline. Re-mark the center front and front fold lines *(white)* with basting *(green)*.

2. Trim the interfacings *(dark gray)*, following the instructions for Facing a Round Neckline, Step 2 *(page 146)*.

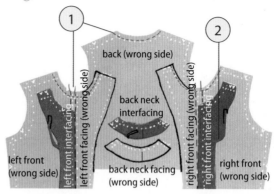

back (wrong side)

left front facing (wrong side)

left front interfacing

back neck interfacing

left front
(wrong side)

back neck facing
(wrong side)

right front facing (wrong side)

right front interfacing

right front
(wrong side)

Attaching the Interfacing to the Garment

3. Adjust the garment for fit and make corresponding adjustments on the interfacing.

4. Pin and baste *(red)* all interfacings to the front and back sections of the garment at the neck along the neck seam-line markings. Be sure to baste only between the seam intersections, not all the way to the ends of the interfacing. Remove the pins.

5. Pin the left and right front interfacings to the corresponding front sections ⅛ inch outside the center front fold line. Baste along the pinned line with thread the same color as the fabric. Make long stitches on the interfacing side but do not stitch through the garment fabric; pick up only a thread of the garment fabric. Begin the basting at the neck seam line and end at the bottom of the garment. Remove the pins.

6. Trim the interfacing around the neckline close to the bastings. Do not trim along the front fold lines.

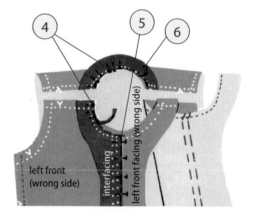

left front
(wrong side)

interfacing

left front facing (wrong side)

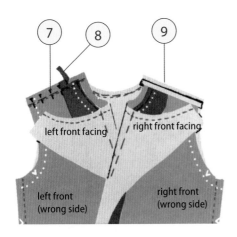

left front facing

right front facing

left front
(wrong side)

right front
(wrong side)

7. With the wrong sides of the fabric facing out, pin and baste the shoulder seams of the garment. Remove the pins, machine stitch along the seam markings, and remove the basting.

8. Trim all interfacings along the shoulder seams ⅛ inch from the stitching.

9. Press the shoulder seams open and trim to ½ inch.

Attaching the Back Neck Facing to the Garment

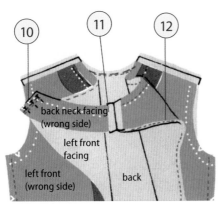

back neck facing
(wrong side)

left front
facing

left front
(wrong side)

back

10. Pin and baste the back neck facing to the front facings along the shoulder seam markings. Remove the pins, machine stitch along the seam markings and remove the basting.

11. Press the seams open and trim to ½ inch.

12. Finish the unnotched edge of the facing as you would any seam *(page 90)*, or fold it over ¼ inch and press. Machine stitch ⅛ inch from the folded edge.

Stitching the Facing and Garment Together

13. Turn the garment right side out. Then fold back the front facings along the front fold lines so that they are wrong side out.

14. Slide the back neck facing, wrong side out, behind the garment back.

15. Pin all facings to the garment along the neck seam line. Match and pin at notches and seam intersections, then at ½-inch intervals in between.

16. Baste along the neck seam line and remove the pins. Machine stitch the neck seam, and remove the basting.

17. Trim the center front corners diagonally, cutting to within ⅛ inch of the stitching.

18. Trim the facings around the neckline to within ⅛ inch of the neckline seam and trim the garment seam to within ¼ inch of the neckline.

19. Clip into all seam allowances at ½-inch intervals around the neck, cutting close but not into the stitching.

20. Turn the garment wrong side out.

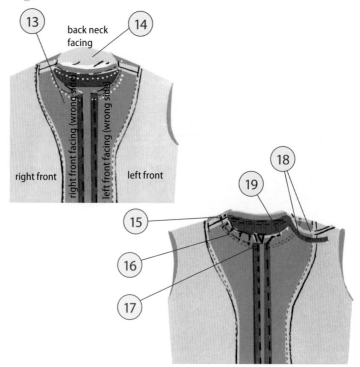

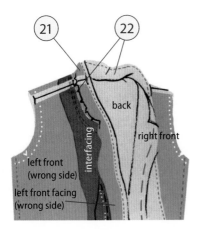

21. Extend the facing away from the garment and press the neckline seam allowances toward the facing.

22. Understitch the facing and seam allowances around the neck as shown for the round neck facing, Step 21 *(page 149)*. Begin and end the understitching 1 inch from the corners as shown.

Hand Finishing the Facing

23. Fold the facing over the wrong side of the garment and press flat.

24. Pin the facing to the garment at the shoulder seams as shown and hand stitch to the shoulder seam allowances with a slip stitch *(black)*. Remove the pins.

25. Remove any remaining bastings and press again.

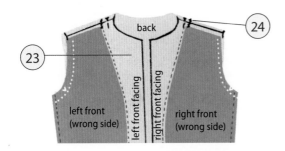

POCKETS

Two of the most common types of pockets are patch and in-seam—one in plain view, the other concealed. The patch pocket may vary widely in shape, depending on the pattern, but it is simply a piece of fabric—usually the same that is used for the garment—stitched along three sides to the outside of the garment. The in-seam pocket—stitched, as its name implies, inside the garment seams—is made of lining fabric, which is thin enough to avoid a telltale bulge. It must be made as a complete unit and then fastened to the side and waistline seams.

Even though the patch pocket is the easiest kind to make, it requires care in positioning. After you have put the pattern markings for the pocket on the body of the garment, try it on to make sure it is conveniently and attractively placed. On a skirt, for instance, the pocket may be too low for you to put your hand in comfortably. Or it may be so far to the side that it overemphasizes the hip. The in-seam pocket offers no options in placement, but if you have let in or taken out the area where the pocket will be inserted, be sure to make a corresponding alteration to the pocket pattern piece.

Preparing the Pocket Section

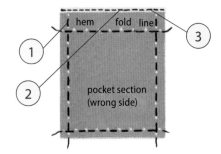

1. Run a basting stitch *(green)* along the pattern markings *(white)* for all the seam lines and the hem fold line.

2. With the pocket section wrong side up, fold down the top hem edge ¼ inch and press.

3. Machine stitch *(blue)* close to the folded hem edge and press again.

Finishing the Hem Edge

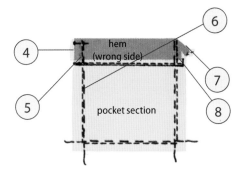

4. Turn the pocket section over, wrong side down. Fold the hem over along the hem fold line and press.

5. Pin and baste *(red)* the hem to the pocket section just outside the basted seam line. Remove the pins.

6. Machine stitch a line along the three seam lines just outside the basted markings. Begin at the folded hem edge and stitch down to the end of the side seam, then stitch across the bottom of the pocket and up the other side seam to the top folded hem edge. Remove all bastings.

7. Trim the two corners of the hem edge diagonally.

8. Trim both side seam allowances of the hem only to ¼ inch.

POCKETS: PATCH POCKETS

Completing Straight Pockets

9a. On pockets with straight bottoms, turn the pocket section wrong side up, turn over the hem and press. Then fold in the side seam allowances just beyond the line of machine stitching made in Step 6 and press. Fold up the bottom seam allowance and press.

Completing Pointed Pockets

9b. On pockets with pointed bottoms, turn the pocket section wrong side up, turn over the hem and press. Then fold up the two bottom seam allowances that form the point just beyond the line of machine stitching made in Step 6; press. Fold in the side seam allowances and press.

Completing Rounded Pockets

9c. On pockets with rounded bottoms, turn the pocket section wrong side up, turn over the hem and press. Notch the curves at ½-inch intervals. Fold in the seam allowances just beyond the machine stitching made in Step 6 and press. Overlap the notched segments where necessary.

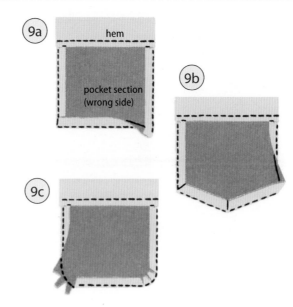

Stitching the Pocket to the Garment

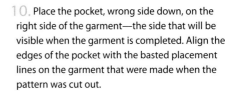

10. Place the pocket, wrong side down, on the right side of the garment—the side that will be visible when the garment is completed. Align the edges of the pocket with the basted placement lines on the garment that were made when the pattern was cut out.

11. Pin the pocket to the garment at each corner and at 1-inch intervals.

12. Baste along the side and bottom edges of the pocket, ¼ inch in from the edges. Remove the pins.

13. Try on the garment and adjust the position of the pocket if necessary.

Invisible Finish

14a. For an invisible finish hand stitch *(black)* the pocket to the garment with a slip stitch *(page 25)*.

Visible Finish

14b. To add strength and give a visible finish, machine stitch the pocket to the garment close to the edge *(Edge Stitching, page 15)*. Add a line of topstitching *(page 15)* if desired.

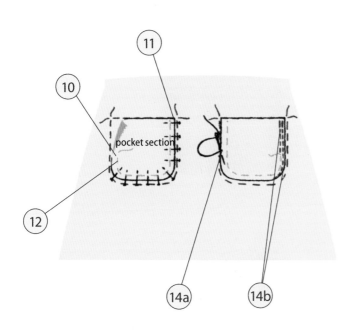

pocket section

Preparing the Pocket Section

1. On the right-hand pocket section—cut out of lining, not garment, fabric—run a line of basting stitches *(green)* along the pattern markings *(white)* for the seam and placement lines.

2. If your pattern includes a marking at the waistline for aligning the pocket with the pants, re-mark it with a vertical running stitch *(page 21)*.

3. Re-mark with a horizontal running stitch the pattern markings for the bottom of the pocket opening.

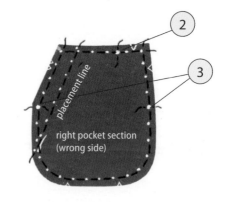

Preparing the Facings

4. Cut a right-hand pocket facing from the garment fabric, using the facing pattern piece, and run a line of basting stitches along the pattern markings for the seam lines.

5. If your pattern includes a marking at the waistline for aligning the pocket with the pants, re-mark it with a vertical running stitch.

6. Re-mark with a horizontal running stitch the pattern markings for the bottom of the pocket opening.

7. Fold over the long unnotched edge of the facing along the basted seam line and press.

8. Trim the pressed edge to ¼ inch and trim the excess fabric from the bottom corner. Remove the basting from the pressed edge.

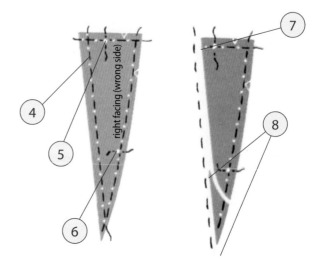

9. Cut a rectangular facing strip from the garment fabric, according to the measurements on your pattern guide sheet.

10. With the facing strip wrong side up, fold over one long edge ¼ inch and press.

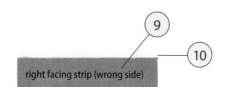

Stitching the Facings to the Pocket

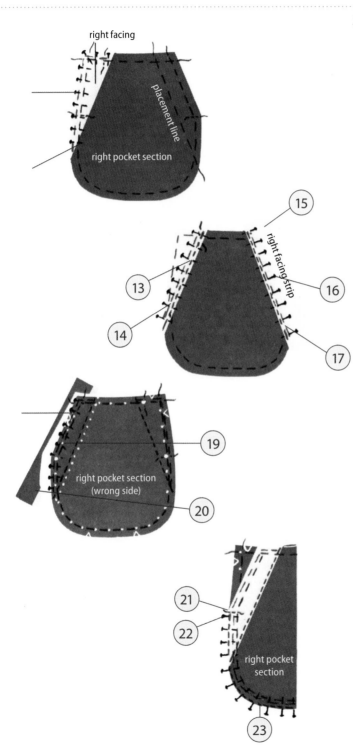

right facing

placement line

right pocket section

right facing strip

right pocket section
(wrong side)

right pocket section

11. Place the right-hand pocket section wrong side down and lay the facing, wrong side down, on it. Pin the facing to the pocket section along the basted seam line, matching the notches and the running-stitch markings.

12. Baste the facing to the pocket section ¼ inch outside the seam markings. Remove the pins.

13. Pin and baste the facing to the pocket along the folded edge made in Step 7. Remove the pins.

14. Machine stitch close to the folded edge. Remove the basting from the folded edge only.

15. Place the facing strip, wrong side down, on the pocket, lining up the folded edge made in Step 10 with the basted placement line on the pocket section.

16. Pin and baste the facing strip to the pocket section along the folded edge. Remove the pins.

17. Machine stitch close to the folded edge. Remove the bastings from the folded edge.

18. Turn the pocket section over, wrong side up, and pin the pocket section to the facing strip along the outer seam-line markings.

19. Baste ¼ inch outside the seam markings. Remove the pins.

20. Trim the facing strip so that it is even with the pocket section around all edges.

Sewing the Pocket

21. Fold the pocket in half lengthwise, wrong sides together, matching pattern markings and the horizontal running stitches marking the pocket opening.

22. Pin and baste the pocket together along the basted seam line from the horizontal running stitch that marks the bottom of the pocket opening *(Step 6)* to the bottom of the folded edge. Remove the pins.

23. Machine stitch the basted seam ¼ inch outside the seam markings.

24. Clip into the seam allowances at the horizontal markings for the bottom of the pocket opening, cutting to the stitching line.

25. Trim the seam allowances to ⅛ inch, cutting from the bottom fold to the clip made in Step 24.

26. Notch around the curve. Then remove all basting from the stitched seam.

27. Turn the pocket wrong side out and press the stitched seam flat.

28. Machine stitch on the seam markings from the clip to the bottom folded edge. Reinforce the seam at the clip by going forward three stitches, back three, then forward to the seam end.

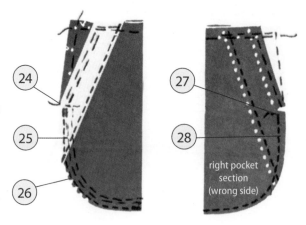

right pocket section (wrong side)

Attaching the Pocket to the Pants

29. Complete the pants up to the point at which both front sections have been stitched together at the crotch, the zipper has been inserted and the outer pants leg seams have been stitched up to the pattern markings for the pocket opening.

30. Lay the pants front wrong side down and lay over it the back section wrong side up. Then fold down the upper portion of the pants back as far as the bottom of the pocket opening.

31. With the right-hand pocket wrong side out, lay it down on the right-hand pants front, matching the notches of the open side edges. The number of notches on the upper part of the pocket (two in this diagram) will correspond to the number of notches on the pants front opening.

32. Push the underneath side of the pocket out of the way.

33. Pin only the upper side of the pocket to the pants front along the side seam line. Insert the first pin at the very bottom of the seam opening. Pin next at the notches and at the intersection of the side seam line with the waist seam line, then at ½-inch intervals in between.

34. Baste the pocket to the pants just outside the side seam line and remove the pins. Then machine stitch along the seam line. Remove the basting.

35. Press open the seam to the bottom of the pocket opening.

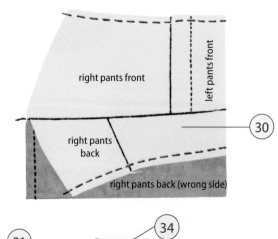

right pants front

left pants front

right pants back

right pants back (wrong side)

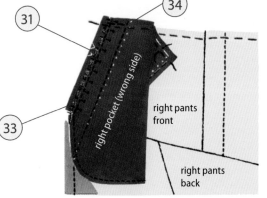

right pocket (wrong side)

right pants front

right pants back

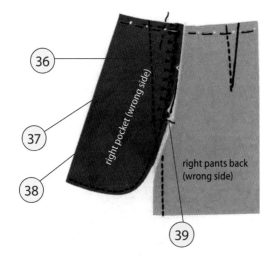

right pocket (wrong side)

right pants back
(wrong side)

36. Fold the pocket over so that it lies outside the pants, and lift up the folded-down pants back.

37. Pin the remaining unstitched side of the pocket to the open portion of the pants back along the side seam line. Pin first at the very bottom of the opening, then at the notches and the intersection of the side seam line with the waist seam line, and finally at ½-inch intervals in between.

38. Baste the pocket to the pants back along the seam line. Remove the pins.

39. Machine stitch the seam. Remove all bastings except the basted marking along the waist seam line. Press open the stitched seam.

Finishing the Pocket

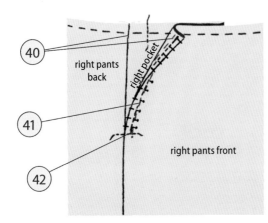

right pants
back

right pocket

right pants front

40. Open the right pants section so it lies flat, wrong side down, and turn the pocket toward the pants front. Press the front pocket seam flat.

41. Pin along the pressed seam to hold it flat, and baste ⅜ inch from the edge.

42. Pushing the rest of the pocket and the pants back fabric out of the way, place the pants front under the machine presser foot. Topstitch (page 15) the front pocket opening seam ¼ inch in from the folded edge, from the waist to the bottom of the pocket opening.

43. Pull the threads to the inside of the pocket and tie them off. Remove the basting.

44. At the waistline, align the front edge of the pocket with the vertical running stitch and pin.

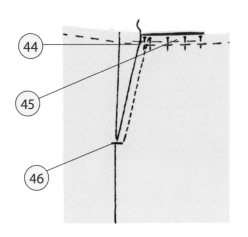

45. Pin the pants front to the folded pocket along the waist seam-line markings, then baste just outside the seam-line markings. Remove the pins.

46. Reinforce the bottom of the pocket opening by machine stitching at right angles to the side seam through all layers of the fabric from the end of the topstitching made in Step 42 to just beyond the side seam. Stitch forward, then backward, then forward again, then pull the threads through to the wrong side of the garment and tie them off. Press.

47. Repeat Steps 1–46 on the left pocket section, facing and strip.

FASTENERS

Buttons, snaps, hooks and eyes are the final professional touch, to be added only after a garment is otherwise finished. Buttons are decorative as well as functional; select them with an eye to the fabric as well as the size of the wearer; for example, small pearl buttons would be inappropriate on a checked tweed dress, and large metallic buttons might overwhelm a tiny figure.

Horizontal buttonholes should be used on close-fitting garments, where there is some stress, vertical buttonholes where there is less strain, such as on a shirt. Once you have adjusted your pattern, reposition buttonholes as shown on pages 164 and 166. But first make a test run with the same fabric and the same number of layers with which you will be working on your garment. For knits, interface the area on which buttonholes will be placed or the fabric will stretch.

Hooks and eyes are best used as hidden fasteners for overlapping edges, such as the waistbands of skirts or pants. Snaps have little holding power and are used to tack down edges invisibly in conjunction with other fasteners.

These instructions are intended for women's garments, which close with the right-hand side over the left. For men's garments, reverse the directions in the instructions.

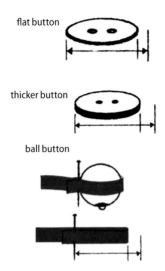

flat button

thicker button

ball button

To find the size of your buttonholes, first measure the buttons to be attached. For a flat, thin button, measure its diameter and add ⅛ inch. For a thicker button, measure its diameter and add ¼ inch. For a mounded or ball button, place a thin strip of paper across the mound or ball, pin it tightly in place, slide the paper off, flatten it, then measure it and add ¼ inch.

FASTENERS: HORIZONTAL BUTTONHOLES

Determining Position

1. To determine the outer placement line for your buttonholes, run basting stitches parallel to and ⅛ inch outside the center front line on the right front of the garment. Use thread of a different color to distinguish this placement line from other basted markings.

2. To determine the inner placement line for your buttonholes, measure in from the outside placement line a distance equal to the size of your buttonhole as established in the box at left. Then make a line of basting stitches parallel to the outer placement line.

3. To space buttonholes, begin at the top. Measure down a distance equal to 1½ times the diameter of your button. Mark with a pin through all layers.

4. To determine the bottom placement line for your buttonholes, measure up from the hemline the distance specified on your pattern. Mark with a pin through all layers.

5. Using pins, space all the intervening buttonholes at equal intervals. Then mark the positions for all the buttonholes with horizontal running stitches *(page 21)* through all layers. To be sure each mark is straight, follow a horizontal grain line in the fabric. If the grain line is difficult to establish, as it would be in tightly woven or synthetic material, mark at right angles to the center front line. The marks should extend about ½ inch beyond either side of the placement lines. Remove the pins.

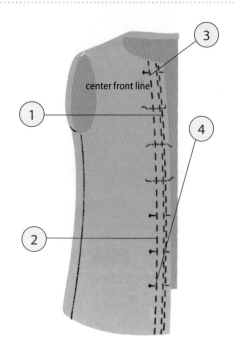

center front line

Making the Buttonhole

6. To make a buttonhole entirely by machine, follow the instructions provided with your particular model. To make a buttonhole without a special accessory, begin halfway between the placement lines and sew tiny machine stitches 1⁄16 inch outside the running stitches that mark the buttonhole position. The stitches should be continuous, pivoting at the corners.

7. With a small pointed scissors, cut the buttonhole along the running stitches, starting in the middle and cutting to each placement line.

8. Sew the buttonhole edges with overcast stitches *(page 27)*, shown in black, to protect them from fraying.

9. Work the overcast edges with a buttonhole stitch *(page 26)*, beginning on the top edge of the buttonhole at the inner placement line.

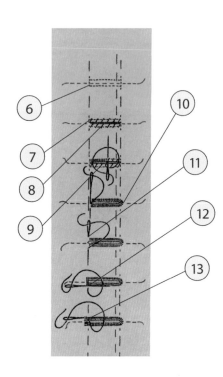

10. At the outer placement line, make five to seven long buttonhole stitches, fanning out about ⅟₁₆ inch beyond the line. Then turn the garment around and repeat for the lower edge. End with a straight vertical stitch at the inner placement line.

11. To finish off the inner edge of the buttonhole with a reinforcement called a bar tack, make three long stitches, side by side, from the top to the bottom edge of the completed rows of buttonhole stitches. These stitches should extend ⅟₁₆ inch beyond the inner placement line.

12. At the bottom edge of the buttonhole, insert the needle horizontally under the three straight stitches made in Step 11, catching the top layer of the fabric underneath. Then pull the needle through, keeping the thread under the needle.

13. Continue to make small stitches across the three long stitches the full depth of the buttonhole.

14. End with two small fastening stitches *(page 28)*.

Placing the Buttons

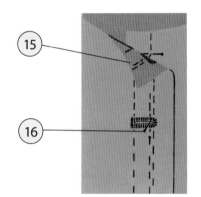

15. Pin the right side of the garment over the left, matching the neck edges of both sides and lining up the basting stitches marking the center front lines.

16. To determine the correct position for the center of each button, insert a pin through each buttonhole at the center front line; the pin should continue through the center front line of the left side of the garment.

17. Mark the position with another pin.

Determining Position

1. To find the size of your buttonholes, first measure the buttons to be attached, following the instructions on page 163.

2. To space your buttonholes begin at the top. Find the upper end of the first buttonhole by measuring down a distance equal to 1½ times the diameter of your button. Mark with a pin through all layers.

3. To find the bottom end of the first buttonhole, measure down from the first pin a distance equal to the size of your buttonhole. Mark with a second pin through all layers.

4. To determine the bottom end of the last buttonhole, measure up from the hemline the distance specified on your pattern. Mark with a pin through all layers.

5. To determine the top end of the last buttonhole, measure up from the first pin a distance equal to the size of your buttonhole. Mark with a pin through all layers.

6. Using pins, space intervening buttonholes at equal intervals. Mark the positions for all the buttonholes with horizontal running stitches *(page 21)*, as indicated in green, through all layers of the garment. The marks should extend about ½ inch on either side of the center front line. Remove the pins.

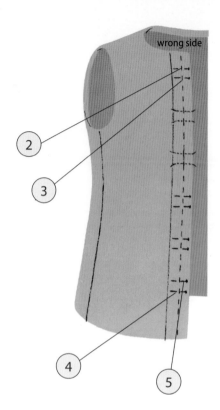

wrong side

Making a Vertical Buttonhole

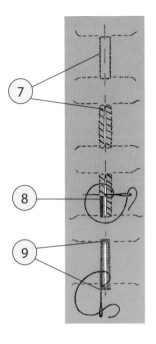

7. To make a buttonhole entirely by machine, follow the instructions provided with your particular model. To make a buttonhole without a special accessory, machine stitch, cut and overcast *(black)* the edges as for the horizontal buttonhole, Steps 6–8 *(page 164)*.

8. Work the overcast edges with a buttonhole stitch *(page 26)*, beginning at the bottom of the inner edge.

9. After completing the inner edge, make a bar tack *(Horizontal Buttonholes, Steps 11–13, page 165)* and continue along the outer edge, finishing off with another bar tack.

10. End with two small fastening stitches *(page 28)*.

Placing Buttons

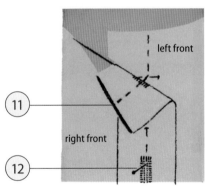

left front

right front

11. Pin the right side of the garment over the left, matching the neck edges and lining up the basting stitches marking the center front lines.

12. To determine the correct position for the center of each button, insert a pin ⅛ inch below the top end of each buttonhole; the pin should continue through the center front line of the garment's left side.

13. Mark this position with another pin.

1. Using a strand of knotted buttonhole twist, make a small stitch in the fabric at the point where the center of the button is to fall. Insert the needle through one of the holes on the underside of the button and pull the thread through.

2. Hold a wooden kitchen match or a toothpick between the button holes and pull the thread over it as you point the needle down into the other hole. Then make two or three stitches across the match; in the case of a four-hole button, make two rows of parallel stitches across the match.

3. Remove the match and pull the button up, away from the fabric, to the top of the threads.

4. Wind the thread five or six times, tightly, around the loose threads below the button to create a thread shank.

5. End by making a fastening stitch *(page 28)* in the thread shank.

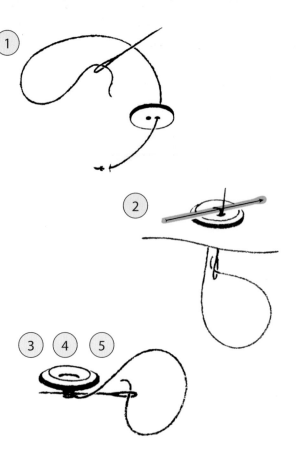

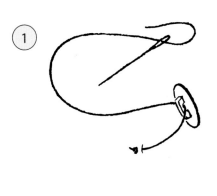

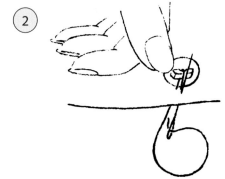

1. Using a strand of knotted buttonhole twist, make a small stitch in the fabric at the point where the center of the button is to fall. Insert the needle through the hole in the shank of the button and pull the thread through.

2. Angle the button away from the fabric with your thumb and take two or three stitches through the button shank.

3. Wind the thread tightly five or six times around the thread shank made in Step 2.

4. End by making a fastening stitch *(page 28)* in the thread shank.

1. Place the half of the snap having a prong or ball in its center on the wrong side of the overlapping part of the garment.

2. Hold the pronged half in place by putting it at the point of closure and about ⅛ inch from the edge to be held in place and inserting a straight pin through the tiny hole inside the prong.

3. Using a double strand of knotted thread, take a small stitch—catching only the inside layer of fabric—through one of the holes and then around the edge of the snap. Tuck the knot under the snap.

4. Take a second stitch at the first hole, then slide the needle under the snap and up through another hole. Repeat until all the holes are completed, and end with two small fastening stitches (page 28) at one edge under the snap.

5. Place the overlap so that the straight pin holding the pronged half in place goes through the underlap. Insert a second pin through the underlap to mark the spot pierced by the first pin.

6. Slide the socket half of the snap onto the second pin and sew it in place as you did in Steps 3 and 4.

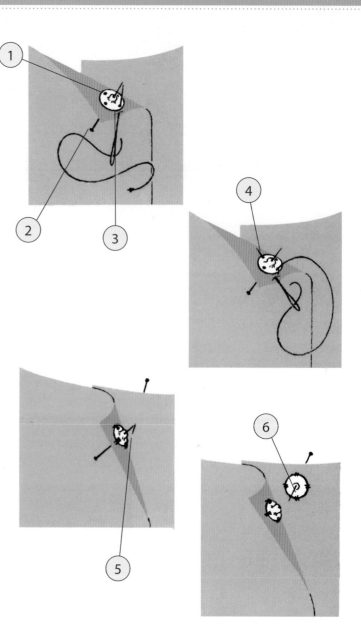

Sewing on Hooks with Rounded Eyes

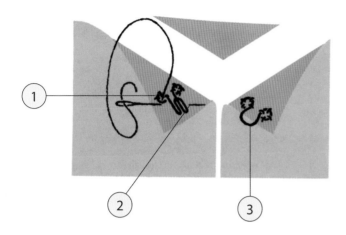

1. When edges meet on the back of garments, place the hook at the left-hand side of the closure, ⅛ inch from the fabric edge. Using a double strand of knotted thread, stitch around each metal ring, catching only the inside fabric layer.

2. Continue by sliding the needle under the hook and take a few stitches over the hook, under the bend. End with a fastening stitch *(page 28)* through the inside layer of fabric.

3. Place the round eye on the right-hand side of the closure so that it protrudes just beyond the edge and the garment edges meet exactly. Sew around each metal ring as in Step 1. End with a fastening stitch.

Sewing on Hooks with Straight Eyes

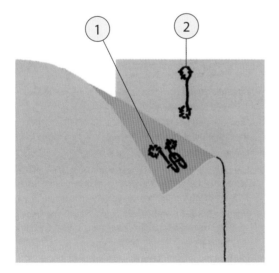

1. On garments where the edges overlap, attach the hook to the overlapping side of the closure, as in Steps 1 and 2 on page 170.

2. Place the overlap so that the bend of the hook falls where the straight eye is to be positioned. Sew the eye in place by stitching around the two metal rings, this time catching all layers of fabric.

Adjustment Line: A double line printed on a pattern piece to indicate where it may be lengthened or shortened.

All-Purpose Foot: See **Presser Foot.**

Bar Tack: A hand-worked trim for reinforcing the ends of buttonholes and other openings.

Baste: To stitch to hold fabric pieces together temporarily, or to indicate pattern markings on both sides of the fabric. Basting stitches can be made by hand or by machine, generally at six stitches per inch.

Bias: A direction diagonal to the threads forming woven fabric—the warp and woof, or "grains." The true bias is at a 45° angle to the grains. Fabric is cut on a bias to make it drape in folds, as in a skirt, or to make it stretch slightly, as in a belt.

Bias Tape: A strip of cotton, cut diagonally to the fabric threads—on the bias—so that it will stretch to cover curved edges of a garment piece. It is available in ¼-inch, ½-inch and 1-inch widths. The 1-inch width has edges folded ¼ inch to the wrong side. It may be single fold, with edges that are folded to the wrong side and meet in the center, or double fold, with an additional fold just off center.

Bobbin: The spool holding the lower of the two threads a sewing machine locks together in a stitch.

Chalk Marker: A gauge used to set skirt lengths. It consists of an adjustable stand holding a rubber bulb that, when squeezed, emits a puff of chalk to mark a hemline.

Clip: A short cut into the fabric outside a seam to help it lie flat around curves and corners.

Closure: The area on which fasteners—such as buttons or zippers—are placed to open and close a garment; also, the fasteners themselves.

Crosswise Grain: See **Grain.**

Cutting Line: A long, unbroken line printed on a pattern, often accompanied by a drawing of scissors, that indicates where it must be cut.

Dart: A stitched fabric fold, tapering to a point at one or both ends, that shapes fabric around curves.

Dressmaker's Carbon: A marking paper, available in several colors and white, used with a tracing wheel to transfer construction lines from pattern to fabric.

Ease: The even distribution of fullness, without forming gathers or tucks, that enables one section of a garment to be smoothly joined to a slightly smaller section, as in the seam joining a sleeve to its armhole.

Ease Allowance: The extra material provided for in patterns to give room in a garment for comfort and ease of movement.

Edge Stitch: Machine stitching on the visible side of the garment, close to the finished edges.

Facing: A piece of fabric, frequently the same as that used in the garment, that covers the raw fabric edge at openings such as necklines and armholes. It is sewn to the visible side of the opening, then turned to the inside so that the seam between it and the garment is enclosed.

Fastener: Any device that opens and closes a garment—button, hook and eye, snap or zipper.

Flat Felled Seam: A double-stitched seam for tailored shirts and slacks in which the seam allowance of one piece forming the seam is trimmed and the seam allowance of the other piece is turned in and stitched on top of the first to give a finished effect on both sides of the garment.

Foot: See **Presser Foot.**

Grading: Trimming each seam allowance within a multilayer seam—the fabric, facing, interfacing, etc.—to a different width to reduce bulk and make the seam lie flat.

Grain: The direction of threads in woven fabrics. The warp—the threads running from one cut end of the material to the other—forms the lengthwise grain. The woof—the threads running across the lengthwise grain from one finished edge of the fabric to the other—forms the crosswise grain. Only if the two grains are at right angles to each other is the fabric aligned on the "true grain."

Grain-Line Arrow: The double-ended arrow printed on a pattern piece indicating how the piece is to be aligned with the threads of the fabric, its grains. The line between the arrow heads must be placed parallel to either the lengthwise or crosswise grain, as specified on the piece.

Guide Sheet: Instructions included with a pattern to provide specific directions for using the pattern pieces to make the garment.

Ham: A ham-shaped cushion used for pressing shaped areas and curves.

Interfacing: A special fabric sewn between two layers of garment fabric to stiffen, strengthen and support parts of the garment. It is usually used around necklines, in collars, cuffs, pockets or waistbands.

Interlining: A special fabric, sewn and shaped exactly like the garment and lining to add warmth.

Lap: To extend one piece of fabric over another, as at the connection of the ends of a belt.

Lengthwise Grain: See **Grain.**

Lining: A fabric, usually lightweight, constructed in the shape of a garment to cover the inside of part or all of the garment. It can also stiffen and strengthen the garment.

Machine Baste: To insert temporary stitching for marking or preliminary seaming, working by machine rather than by hand. For basting, the machine is set at six stitches per inch.

Mercerizing: A chemical treatment for cotton fabric and thread to add strength and luster, and make the material more receptive to dye.

Nap: The short fibers on the surface of the fabric that have been drawn out and brushed in one direction, such as on velvet or corduroy.

Notch: A V- or diamond-shaped marking made on the edge of a garment piece as an alignment guide. It is meant to be matched with a similar notch or group of notches on another piece when the two pieces are joined.

Notions: Supplies used in sewing—needles, thread, pins, buttons, zippers, etc.

Overlap: The part of the garment that extends over another part, as at the opening of a blouse, jacket or waistband.

Pattern Layout and Cutting Guide: The instructions and diagrams showing how to place the pattern pieces on the fabric for cutting.

Pile: See **Nap**.

Pinking: A serrated edge at a seam, produced by special "pinking" shears to prevent woven fabrics from raveling.

Placement Line: A line printed on a pattern to indicate where buttonholes, pockets, trimming and pleats are to be placed.

Placket: A garment opening with an overlapping edge covered by a visible strip of fabric running the length of the opening. It is used with openings that are equipped with fasteners.

Pleats: Folds of fabric used to control fullness.

Pre-Shrink: A chemical treatment that prevents fabric in the garment from shrinking when it is washed or dry-cleaned. If fabric is not labeled "pre-shrunk," it should be washed, if it is washable, or pre-shrunk by a dry cleaner.

Presser Foot: The part of a sewing machine that holds fabric steady at the point it is being advanced and the needle is stitching it. The "all-purpose," or general-purpose, foot has two prongs, or "toes," of equal length, and is used for most stitching. The "straight-stitch" foot has one long and one short toe, and can be used for straight stitching and stitching over fabrics of varying thicknesses. The "zipper" foot has only one toe and is used to stitch zippers and cording.

Reinforce: To strengthen an area that will be subjected to strain, such as the bottom of a pocket, with a small patch of fabric or extra stitches.

Seam: The joint between two or more pieces of fabric, or the line of stitching that makes a fold in a single piece of fabric, such as a dart.

Seam Allowance: The extra fabric—usually ⅝ inch—that extends outside the seam line.

Seam Binding: Ribbon, ½ inch or 1 inch wide, of rayon, silk or nylon, that is sewn over fabric edges to cover them, concealing their raw appearance and preventing raveling. Seam binding is also available cut diagonally to the fabric threads—on the bias—to sew over curved edges. See also **Bias Tape**.

Seam Finish: The treatment of raw seam edges to prevent fraying and raveling.

Seam Line, also called stitching line: The long broken line printed on a pattern to indicate where a seam must be stitched; it is usually ⅝ of an inch inside the cutting line.

Selvage: The finished edges on woven fabric.

Shank: The link between the button and the fabric to which it is sewn. The shank can be made with thread or it can be part of the button, but it must be long enough to allow for the thickness of the overlapping fabric.

Slash: A long, straight cut to make a garment opening or to open a fold of fabric so that it will lie flat, reducing bulkiness.

Sleeve Board: Two small ironing boards of different widths, connected at one end, for pressing garment areas (such as sleeves) that will not fit over a regular ironing board.

Stay Stitch: A line of machine stitches sewn at 12 stitches per inch on the seam line of a garment piece before the seam is stitched. Stay stitching is used as a reinforcement to prevent curved edges from stretching, and as a guide for folding an edge accurately.

Stitching Line: See **Seam Line**.

Straight-Stitch Foot: See **Presser Foot**.

Synthetic Fibers: Man-made fibers produced by forming filaments from chemical solutions, such as rayon, nylon and Dacron.

Take-Up Lever: The lever on the sewing machine that raises and lowers the presser foot.

Tension: The degree of tightness of the two threads forming machine stitches. Unless tension is properly adjusted in each, the threads will not lock evenly together in the stitch.

Thread: Twisted strands of yarn used for sewing.

Throat Plate: A flat metal piece with a hole through which the needle passes as it stitches. A general-purpose throat plate has a wide hole to accommodate sideways motion of the needle; many machines also have a second throat plate with a small hole, to prevent soft fabrics and knits from being pulled down into the machine and puckering during stitching. Throat plates have guide lines on the left and right sides to help you sew a straight seam.

Topstitch: A line of machine stitching on the visible side of the garment parallel to a seam.

Tracing Wheel: A small wheel attached to a handle, used in conjunction with dressmaker's carbon to transfer markings from pattern pieces to fabric. Tracing wheels with serrated edges are used for most fabrics, but plain edges are preferred for knits to avoid snagging the material.

Trim: To cut away excess fabric in the seam allowance after the seam has been stitched. Also, a strip of fabric—such as braid or ribbon—used to decorate a garment.

Underlap: A part of a garment that extends under another part, as at the connection at the ends of a belt.

With Nap: A cutting direction on patterns to indicate how the pattern is to be aligned with fabrics that, because of their surface, napped weave or printed design, change in appearance with the direction in which they are set. When such fabrics are used, all pattern pieces must be laid and cut out in one direction—with the nap.

Zigzag Stitch: A serrated line of machine stitching used as decoration or to prevent raveling of raw edges, particularly on knits.

Zipper: Sometimes called slide fastener: A mechanical fastener consisting of two tapes holding parallel lines of teeth or coils that can be interlocked by a sliding bracket, or slider. The zipper generally has a top stop, a small metal bracket or bit of stitching at the top to prevent the slider from running off the tapes; a guide line, a raised line woven into the tapes to show where they are to be stitched to the garment; and a bottom stop, a bracket at the bottom against which the slider rests when the zipper is open.

Zipper Foot: See **Presser Foot**.

INDEX

Discover these other great craft books from Fox Chapel Publishing

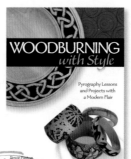

DISCARDED BY FREEPORT MEMORIAL LIBRARY